rib

Encountering Assyria's great
and terrifying ruler

CLIVE ANDERSON

ERIES EDITOR: SIMON J ROBINSON

DayOne

© Day One Publications 2007

First printed 2007

ISBN 978-1-84625-076-7

ISBN 978–1–84625–076–7

British Library Cataloguing in Publication Data available

Published by Day One Publications
Ryelands Road, Leominster, HR6 8NZ
Telephone 01568 613 740   FAX 01568 611 473

email—sales@dayone.co.uk
web site—www.dayone.co.uk

Designed by Steve Devane and printed by Gutenberg Press, Malta.

For
Kathy and Mark
Charles and Sandra

Clive Anderson brings ancient history to life. Out of the stony slabs of antiquity, Sennacherib emerges, flesh and blood. Using biblical sources and drawing on his extensive knowledge of archaeology and ancient history, Clive Anderson gives the reader a fascinating insight into the life and times of this notorious Assyrian king—enriching and sharpening our understanding of the biblical text. This book is a must for preachers and teachers and an invaluable aid to Bible study. It is easily accessible scholarship—providing accurate background knowledge, sound biblical exposition and searching application.

Rev. Dr Jim Winter, Pastor, Horsell Evangelical Church, and author of several books

Clive Anderson brings two great passions to bear in the writing of this book. The first is that by filling in the blanks of our map of Old Testament history the key points which God highlights would be better seen and understood by God's people. The second is that from a clearer understanding of God's dealings with his people would flow a clearer desire to walk in God's ways. Both passions are plain to see throughout this book and applied with insight and wisdom by a very knowledgeable and passionate writer.

Chris Hughes, Pastor of Bishopstoke Evangelical Church, Hampshire, England

Contents

THE DESTRUCTION OF SENNACHERIB

LORD BYRON (FIRST PUBLISHED IN 1815)
The Assyrian came down like the wolf on the fold,
And his cohorts were gleaming in purple and gold;
And the sheen of their spears was like stars on the sea,
When the blue wave rolls nightly on deep Galilee.

Like the leaves of the forest when Summer is green,
That host with their banners at sunset were seen:
Like the leaves of the forest when Autumn hath blown,
That host on the morrow lay withered and strown.

For the Angel of Death spread his wings on the blast,
And breathed in the face of the foe as he passed;
And the eyes of the sleepers waxed deadly and chill,
And their hearts but once heaved, and for ever grew still!

And there lay the steed with his nostril all wide,
But through it there rolled not the breath of his pride;
And the foam of his gasping lay white on the turf,
And cold as the spray of the rock-beating surf.

And there lay the rider distorted and pale,
With the dew on his brow, and the rust on his mail:
And the tents were all silent, the banners alone,
The lances unlifted, the trumpet unblown.

And the widows of Ashur are loud in their wail,
And the idols are broke in the temple of Baal;
And the might of the Gentile, unsmote by the sword,
Hath melted like snow in the glance of the Lord!

1 Who are you?

2 Kings 18:13; 2 Chronicles 32:1; Isaiah 36:1

Sennacherib bursts onto the pages of the Bible with the same force as Elijah (1 Kings 17), but unlike that great prophet he was full of menace and evil intent.[1] He was one of the most powerful monarchs in the history of the world, inheriting a vast empire from his father King *Sargon* II (Isaiah 20:1).

Sennacherib was the apogee of Assyrian kingship, and the most prominent ruler of the neo-Assyrian empire. Today he is best known from the biblical account of his campaign in Judah (2 Kings 18–19; 2 Chronicles 32; Isaiah 36–37), which is corroborated by the reliefs that have been discovered in his 'palace without rival' at Nineveh, and because of Lord Byron's famous poem 'The destruction of Sennacherib'.

INTO THE WORLD

In the Akkadian language of his day, Sennacherib's name is *Sin-anhe-eriba*, meaning 'Sin (moon god) has replaced his brothers'. The Assyrians did not keep birth certificates, nor did they leave any records of the ages of kings at death, so it is not known when Sennacherib was born, but it probably occurred somewhere between 740 and 735 BC, therefore he would have been in his forties when he first enters the Old Testament. He was brought up in the 'house of succession', and as his name implies was not the heir but probably the spare, and that those above him had died or had been moved to one side. He was entrusted early in life with considerable administrative and military responsibilities, especially on the northern frontier where, on behalf of his father, he joined a delegation to the court of the fabled King Midas (he of the golden touch, according to later Greek and Roman authorities).

Sennacherib ascended the throne of Ashur (the chief god, sometimes spelt Assur), on the twelfth day of Ab (July-August) 705 BC, and ruled for twenty-four years until 681 BC.

MEET THE FAMILY

Little is known of Sennacherib's family life, although we know his wife was the celebrated *Naqi'a-Zakutu,* a western Semitic. Intriguingly she may have been of Jewish decent, her family being brought into exile by a previous king. This fact makes it clear that Sennacherib, king of an empire of many races, had no racial prejudices when it came to choosing a consort. She was a formidable lady who enhanced the prospects of her son *Esarhaddon* after the death of the crown prince *Ashur-nadin-sumi* in Susa. She was to become not only the queen mother, but also a grandmother of *Ashurbanipal*, the last great king of Assyria. Other women may also have been formally linked to Sennacherib, for polygamy was not forbidden, but a first wife was not to be neglected in favour of the second wife.

Another lady, *Tasmetum-sarret,* is also known from inscriptions, one being a paean of praise to her inscribed by Sennacherib on a bull colossi in the domestic quarters of his palace. But whether she was the second wife or just a favourite of the king and the mother of the crown prince, Ashur-nadin-sumi, it is as yet not possible to tell.

Like many other oriental monarchs, Sennacherib had numerous concubines and quite a number of sons, and it is likely that the ambitions of these concubines' sons were a factor in the power struggle which followed the death of their father. It was to be Esarhaddon, the son of Naqi'a-Zakutu, who eventually succeeded to the throne.

SENNACHERIB'S CV

The stone portraits of Sennacherib present a cold and austere image of a once living man. It is difficult to get a glimpse of the personality of an Assyrian king, but in the case of Sennacherib little hints come through from his many inscriptions.

He enjoyed campaigning, not just for the fighting but also for the opportunity it gave him to go mountaineering:

I, like a strong wild-ox, went before them. Gullies, mountain torrents and waterfalls, dangerous cliffs, I surmounted in my sedan chair. Where it was too steep for my chair, I advanced on foot. Like a young gazelle I mounted the high peaks in pursuit of them. Wherever my knees gave out, I sat down on [some] mountain boulder and drank the cold water from the water skin [to quench] my thirst.

From an inscription of Sennacherib recording his fifth campaign against the hill tribes east of the Tigris.

However, it would have been others who had to carry his chair and supplies as it was not seemly for the king to bear any loads.

AN ALL-ROUNDER

Sennacherib was more than a warrior-king, he was essentially a practical man, interested in improving ways of doing things and in finding new resources to enhance his empire. This was a rare gift in the ancient Near East where the great obstacle to progress was tradition. He was prepared to be an innovator, to seek for new sources of materials and to devise new ways of doing things. An example of the novelty of his attitude can be seen when there was a problem regarding adequate timber supplies. It was a matter of scribal knowledge that certain trees were associated with particular mountains, and this was set out in a traditional list. But the list was copied and recopied simply as a matter of scribal duty, long after some of the mountains listed had become deforested and the identity of others forgotten. The king, however, when he needed large amounts of timber, actually sent surveyors out into the mountains to look for new sources of the various species required.

Similarly, he took deliberate steps to find new sources of various kinds of ornamental stone. When he wanted to cast large bronze statues for a new palace, he tells us that while former kings had had great trouble in doing this, he thought the problem over and devised a more efficient method, maybe with a little help from his friends, but modesty forbids him from mentioning that!

Sennacherib also introduced cotton—'*the wool-bearing tree*'—to Assyria. He personally took part in the search for suitable mountain springs to be tapped and led down by canals to Nineveh. In the canal system which he created to bring water to Nineveh, he devised a means by which 'The sluice-gate of the canal opened by itself without the help of spade or shovel'. He prided himself upon these achievements as much as upon his military conquests, lauding himself as:

the one who digs canals, opens wells, makes the ditches murmur with running water, brings abundance and prosperity to the widespread plough lands of Assyria, who furnishes irrigation waters for the fields of Assyria where no one had seen canals and mechanical irrigation in Assyria from days of old, and which none of those of former times had known or made.

As king he involved himself in the mundane as well as the spectacular, and managed to find time to consider the cultivation of corn and the vine. He devoted his attention to the best methods of storing wine, and sought to

prevent oil, which is the life of man and heals wounds, from rising in price, and the cost of sesame from exceeding that of wheat.

SOCIAL WORK

In addition to the progressive attitudes already mentioned, Sennacherib seems to have had a social conscience, regarding himself as the protector of justice, and by ancient standards he made good this claim. After putting down a revolt in Ekron, he took steps to distinguish between actual rebels, who were executed, and citizens who had taken no active part, who were pardoned. He considered it his duty to defend the weak, and described himself as: 'the one who renders assistance and comes to the help of the destitute'.

THE PEOPLE HE RULED

From the middle of the second millennium BC, Assyria emerged as an aggressive military power proclaiming Ashur as its god.

The land of the Assyrians was in upper Mesopotamia, now in modern-day Iraq. Mesopotamia was the ancient Greek name for the 'land between the two rivers', the Tigris and the Euphrates, with Nineveh, which was to become Sennacherib's capital, situated adjacent to the Tigris. In the north of this country lay snow-clad mountains descending into a mixture of desert and lowland alluvial plain where the four great cities Ashur, Arbil, Nimrud and Nineveh were situated.

Assyria was perhaps the most consistently powerful and most feared nation of all in the ancient world. The Assyrians were brilliant mathematicians, astronomers, engineers and warriors, yet the men from the land of Ashur struck fear into many hearts. Cruelty and terror were certainly weapons in the Assyrian military arsenal.

AS SLIPPERY AS OSAMA BIN LADEN

After the terrorist attacks on the property of the United States in 2001, the Saudi Arabian, Osama Bin Laden, was singled out as public enemy number one. Yet his capture has proved, to date, to be difficult to achieve because he is so elusive.

Sennacherib too was faced with an enemy who proved to be just as hard to pin down in the early years of his reign. For in 703 BC, one of the Chaldaean tribal leaders, Merodach-Baladan (*Marduk-apla-iddina II*), with help from Elam rebelled against Assyrian rule. Sennacherib responded to this threat and a vicious campaign was fought which resulted in temporary success, but he failed to capture Merodach-Baladan and was forced to deal with him at a later date.

RESOLVING CHRONOLOGY

Merodach-Baladan appears in the Bible after Hezekiah has recovered from illness, and is called 'son of Baladan, king of Babylon' (2 Kings 20:12). The passages in 2 Kings 20:1–11 and Isaiah 38 and 39 occur before the invasion of Sennacherib in 2 Kings 18 and 19, and Isaiah 36 and 37. The order is reversed in the Bible for reasons of theology. The narrative runs from the greater to the lesser, from national to individual salvation, to clearly show that if God can and does save his people, then the security of the individual should not be called into question.

Chronologically the salvation of Hezekiah comes before that of Judah (Isaiah 38:6), and he is promised fifteen more years of life. As he died in 687 BC this means that his salvation happened in 702 BC, a year before Sennacherib arrived.

When he recovered from his illness, Merodach-Baladan sent gifts and presents to bolster his alliance against Assyria, something that would not have gone unnoticed in the corridors of power at Nineveh (2 Kings 20:12–13; Isaiah 39:1–2).

ON THE MOVE

To maintain a firm grip on his empire, each year the Assyrian king had to be ready to move against any malcontents or to set out to enlarge his people's territory.

The Bible places the Assyrians as the descendants of Asshur, the second son of Shem and a grandson of Noah (Genesis 10:22). Some of the best-known names from the Assyrian empire are found in the Old Testament. The Assyrian empire was at the height of its power during the eighth and seventh centuries BC. The kings of Judah at this time were Uzziah (ruled 767 to 739 BC) to Hezekiah (ruled 716 to 687 BC).

After his campaign in Babylonia, Sennacherib turned his attention to the west, particularly the land of Judah and its rebellious king Hezekiah. He may have thought that Hezekiah's recent illness would have weakened his resolve. Also, the gifts Hezekiah had received from Babylon meant that Sennacherib needed to quash any further diplomatic missions before they rebounded on him.

FOR FURTHER STUDY

1. The ancient Assyrians appear many times in the Old Testament. Read, note and consider the things that are said about them in the books of Hosea, Jonah, Micah, Nahum, Zephaniah and Zechariah.
2. How should Isaiah 19:23 be interpreted and what implications does it have for the people of God?

TO THINK ABOUT AND DISCUSS

1. Sennacherib was a very important monarch in the ancient world. How helpful is it to learn something of his background to flesh out the Bible?
2. If other items regarding a person in the Bible are not recorded, does that mean that the Bible authors think that it is pointless doing background study for them or did they work to a different agenda?
3. Are there other Bible characters that you would like to know more about? If so, who are they and why would you like more information about them?

Note

1   See **Simon J. Robinson,** *Face2face Elijah* (Leominster: Day One, 2006).

2 Shock and awe

2 Kings 18:13; 2 Chronicles 32:1; Isaiah 36:1

Israel, the Northern Kingdom, and Judah, the Southern Kingdom (the twelve tribes split as a result of civil war after the death of King Solomon) were squeezed between the extremes of the Assyrian empire to the north and east and Egypt to the south.

A DESPERATE SITUATION

In Israel, Jeroboam had built his own religious shrines at Dan and Bethel, and the nation moved in the direction of increasing idolatry and apostasy (2 Kings 12:26–32). After intrigues, assassinations and a four-year civil war within the Northern Kingdom, a new dynasty was founded under Omri who made Samaria his capital. After him, his son Ahab takes over as king of the north, and it is at this point that the ministry of Elijah begins (1 Kings 17). Ahab's reign ended in 853 BC, followed by Jehoram and in 843 BC by Jehu. The prophet Elisha had anointed Jehu as the one who would purge the nation of the pagan cults, which he subsequently did to devastating effect.

While this is happening, the great Assyrian empire is emerging as a superior power that begins to dominate all the other little kingdoms. The smaller nations, worried by this tremendous war machine, start to build alliances against this power to the north. At this point the ministries of two prophets to the Northern Kingdom, Amos and Hosea, were being carried out.

ISRAEL IS NO MORE

Reacting violently to these alliances, *King Tiglath-Pileser III* (sometimes called Pul, which may have been his birth name [2 Kings 15:19], arrived in Northern Israel in 733 BC. This ferocious sovereign captured all the towns of Galilee, including Hazor, deporting a large percentage of the population back to Assyria. He continued campaigning and reached Gaza on the Egyptian border bringing destruction wherever he went, before returning home. The following year he returned to annexe Syria.

Assyrian records show that Israel's King Hoshea (ruled 732–723 BC) was Tiglath-Pileser's puppet and had been put on the throne to maintain Assyrian rule. However, the next Assyrian king, *Shalmaneser V,* learned of a plot against him, for Hoshea was writing to Egypt for help to throw off the Assyrian yoke. Being less then pleased, he brought the full force of his might against Israel in 724 BC and laid siege to Samaria. The city amazingly held out for two years. But the inevitable happened, and the next Assyrian king, Sargon II (Sennacherib's father), completed the military victory and dragged the last king of Israel off in chains, along with many thousands of Israelite subjects.

Between 732 and 721 BC, the 'ten lost tribes' of Israel were deported into the land of the Mitannians, the Meads and Assyria proper (Isaiah 7:13–8:10).

Sargon repeopled the empty towns of Samaria with a

diverse group from Babylon and Hamath, for logic dictated that if they could not understand each other then they could not form an alliance against Assyria. Eventually these became assimilated with a number of Hebrews who returned and they became known as the Samaritans in the New Testament (John 4).

LOOK SOUTH

After Israel had been annexed in 721 BC, the kings of Judah sought to make political alliances rather than to trust in God's promises. Isaiah was the prophet in the south during this period and he was based in Jerusalem. He ministered during the reigns of four kings, in particular King Ahaz and his son, Hezekiah. These two kings play important roles in the book of Isaiah.

When Ahaz died, Hezekiah immediately began a series of pious reforms, dismantling the high places of worship where the Asherah and other sacred poles were positioned (Exodus 34:13). Those high places were a curse to God's people and the Psalmist challenged them when he wrote, 'I lift my eyes to the hills—where does my help come from?' The high places with idolatrous images? No! 'My help comes from the LORD, the Maker of heaven and earth' (Psalm 121:1–2). During this purge, Hezekiah bravely smashed the famed bronze serpent of Moses because it had become an idol (2 Kings 18:4). Continuing his reforms of the land, Hezekiah defeated the Philistines, moving through their territories down to Gaza (2 Kings 18:7–8); God was with him in his endeavours. A deliberate contrast is made between his faith and the faithless behaviour of Israel which resulted in their defeat and deportation (compare 2 Kings 18:5–7 with 2 Kings 18:11–12).

The situation changed when Hezekiah heard that Sargon II, king of Assyria, had died and that great swathes of the Assyrian empire simmered with revolt. Instead of listening to Isaiah he made a tactical error and joined with some of the city-states of the Phoenician (modern-day Lebanon) and Philistine (modern-day West Bank, from Gaza upwards) coasts in an anti-Assyrian league backed by Egypt (Isaiah 30:1–5).

OFF TO WAR

According to 2 Samuel 11:1, 'In the spring, at the time when kings go off to war' (cc 1 Chronicles 20:1) it was the occasion when countries and kingdoms anxiously awaited to discover if they were in for a hard time. Winter with its harsh weather would not have been conducive to marching out, so it was spent in preparing for any forthcoming campaign, and that is what Sennacherib did in the winter of 702–1 BC.

Assyria had a fearsome army; its success lay in forward planning, the quality of its troops, rigid discipline and superior weapons.

Sennacherib brought his formidable host, made up not just of troops but all the ancillary staff needed to keep an army on the move—cooks, engineers, doctors, and many others—with him when he invaded the land. He came down the eastern Mediterranean coast, the route having been described in advance (Isaiah 10:28–31), before proceeding to subjugate the country piecemeal, city by city. Eventually the terrifying force arrived at Lachish, the second most important city in Judah, twenty-five miles south west of Jerusalem. This strategic city had been fought over throughout its history, for command of it guaranteed rule over the trade routes it protected as it acted as a buffer zone between Egypt and the northern kingdoms (Joshua 10:32; Nehemiah 11:30).

A MAGNIFICENT DISCOVERY

In 1851 the young Englishman, Austin Henry Layard, excavating at the ancient site of Nineveh, opposite Mosul in modern Iraq, opened up room 36 of Sennacherib's Palace without Rival, in the mound called Kuyunjik. The four walls of the room were covered with magnificent carved slabs—eighteen metres of them are now in the British Museum in London—depicting the brutal siege of the city of Lachish in Judah. Layard's discovery caused great excitement in the Victorian world as this was the first archaeological conformation of an event from the Bible (2 Kings 18:13–14).

These priceless carvings bring to life siege warfare in the ancient world, for they brilliantly portray the events recorded in the Bible, and are the nearest thing to a series of photographs of an historical scene from the time of Isaiah. Here is visual evidence on a grand scale of the Assyrian army at work and war.

A CUNNING PLAN

The Assyrians did not become a conquering nation by sitting back and letting everything happen around them. Skilled in the art of warfare, the army had developed a four-fold attack plan which had been honed into a fine art when tackling a fortified stronghold. It was *isolation, preparation, penetration* and *suppression.*

• *ISOLATION*

When laying siege to a city they would seek to isolate the city to stop any outside help coming to their aid, so roads or highways would be blocked, rivers patrolled and escape routes nullified.

We can imagine the sense of panic spreading throughout the city as they heard the war drums with their terrifying beat sounding like the sound of distant thunder heralding the coming assault.

• *PREPARATION*

The approach to the defence walls was prepared by levelling the ground to enable the assault troops greater flexibility and manoeuvrability, and to bring into position the machines of war.

• *PENETRATION*

A full-blooded assault on a city when the fighting would have been brutal in the extreme, where few caught up in the mayhem of battle could expect mercy to be shown or given.

• *SUPPRESSION*

After these things the Assyrian army would then seek to suppress the defenders by superior numbers, employing the maximum concentration of firepower.

LET BATTLE COMMENCE

Some time before dawn, sleepy men would have been prodded awake, and the campfires doused, for the coming day would probably be very warm. The Lachish carvings show grapes and figs on the trees indicating that the attack took place in late summer, a simple but useful detail for dating Sennacherib's activities.

After a simple but filling breakfast the assailants would have been arranged in their attack formations. At the appointed time, conversation died away and then the order would have been given to advance. What dread must have filled both the aggressor and defender as they thought of the agony, blood and death to be inflicted before victory came?

Among the solders of the Assyrian army, different nationalities are represented, including some Israelites captured and forced into battle and Iranians with skirts below their knees, these having been pressed into service from previous campaigns. There are ranks of archers, with quivers stuffed with arrows, firing over the walls into the city; some kneel, protected by the tall leather shields of the javelin throwers. Behind them are the bearded artillerymen with long pointed helmets wielding their slings and carrying a spare stone in their left hands; they keep up a barrage of small but lethal missiles, reminiscent of the Bible's account of David's fight with Goliath (1 Samuel 17).

As the battle moves into its next stage, storm troopers with flat helmets are scaling the walls. Excavations at Lachish reveal that there were two outer walls, which must have been a surprise to the besieging Assyrians as usually smaller cities had only one. This is a reminder of the defence systems that Hezekiah put in place at Jerusalem when he knew Sennacherib was coming (2 Chronicles 32:5).

Firing arrows to form a protective shield as they advance, the air is thick with missiles. The siege-engines (five are depicted on the reliefs) with a great spear protruding from the front trundle up the earth and stone ramps to the walls of the city. Archaeologists have discovered that the soldiers of Lachish also built a ramp to counteract the Assyrians, and that they had lowered great chains over the wall from inside the city in the hope that a siege engine would trundle over it so that a violent pull on the chain would upend the vehicle.[1] The historian Adam Hart-Davis has replicated one of these siege engines in a television programme called *What the Ancients did for us*. He proved that they were terrifically powerful and effective and it would not have been easy to stop their destructive progress.

Remains of the great Assyrian ramp have been discovered. It would undoubtedly have been constructed by those captured by the Assyrians in Judah and further afield, for it is less likely that the defenders of Lachish would fire on their own people, though in desperation that may not have been the case. The main siege ramp contains between 13,000 to 19,000 tons of rubble, and would have taken considerable time to construct.

LACHISH FIGHTS BACK BUT TO NO AVAIL

As the sound of battle fills the air, the defenders are desperately hurling their firebombs and rocks upon the attackers; some soldiers are falling over the wall, victims of advancing archers. At the bottom of one panel there is the gruesome scene of prisoners from previous battles, or those who tried to escape the city being impaled alive on long stakes in the sight of the defenders.

Despite the valiant attempts of the defenders, all is in vain and the city falls amidst smoke, fire and carnage. Groups of men and women, with children clinging to their mothers, are led away as prisoners; the spoils of war follow them on camels and in heavily laden ox carts. The leaders of the city are spread-eagled and flayed (skinned) alive, while others are summarily executed.

Usually, the skins of the unfortunate victims were then fixed to a prominent place on the remaining city wall as a warning to all that rebellion would not be tolerated. Watching this horrendous spectacle, the Assyrian artist has depicted a number of children holding onto adults—they obviously believed that a lesson learnt early would not be quickly forgotten (Proverbs 22:6).

NOTHING NEW UNDER THE SUN

Viewing these carvings would have given a sense of danger, tangible yet distant, an attack in the past with future threat.

When the twin towers of the World Trade Centre in New York were attacked by terrorists on 9/11, images of that dreadful event were instantaneously beamed all over the world. For many the morbid fascination of the unfolding drama proved irresistible, for it was happening in real time, with horrific footage of people falling from the upper storeys. Yet it was at a distance, and many were grateful that they were not caught up in the unfolding tragedy. Underlying all though was a sense of future danger, the perpetrators sending out a clear message: we will strike again, and next time it might be personal.

The Lachish reliefs carry the same tangible messages; you are observing the action and can almost smell the blood, sweat and tears. But it is at a distance—this portrayal was originally placed many hundreds of miles away on display in Nineveh.

Yet undergirding it all is future danger—visitors to Sennacherib's palace were left in no doubt that resistance to the Assyrian yoke would not be tolerated and they might be next!

WHY DID LACHISH SUFFER SO APPALLINGLY?

Lachish, the second city of Judah, was brutally destroyed. The remains of fifteen hundred men, women and children buried in a mass grave have been discovered. Undoubtedly a great number were also dragged off into exile, and some appear as slaves on Sennacherib's other wall carvings at Nineveh, notably in the transportation of a colossal bull statue.

The prophet Micah leaves no doubt as to the reason for the suffering and capitulation of the city; it was the judgement of God.

'You who live in Lachish, harness the team to the chariot. You were the beginning of sin to the Daughter of Zion, for the transgressions of Israel were found in you' (Micah 1:13). The sin of Lachish affected the rest of the land and it is salutary to remember that no one sins in isolation, for an individual sin always affects others in one way or another.

FOR FURTHER STUDY

1. In 2 Kings 6:24–33 a previous siege at Samaria is described in graphic detail. Read it to learn how awful it was and also to see how desperately people behave when they are hungry.
2. Jesus predicted that Jerusalem would fall and great atrocities would take place. Read his words in Matthew 24:1–35.

TO THINK ABOUT AND DISCUSS

1. *Brutality often follows on from a battle situation. Do you think it is difficult for Christians who serve in the armed forces to show restraint when the spoils of war are being claimed?*
2. *Is it ever right for a Christian to take up arms against another person or country? What verses in the Bible can you turn to in support of your argument, either for or against war and violence?*
3. *The history of Israel is fascinating if complicated, but how can knowledge of what has happened in the past help in understanding the present situation?*
4. *Isaiah 11:6–9 describes the golden age to come when wars will be a thing of the past. Do you think this is poetic licence or future reality?*

Note

1   **Philip J. King,** *Biblical Archaeology Review*, volume 31, number 4, July/August 2005, p. 36.

3 Diplomatic talk

2 Kings 18:17–37; 2 Chronicles 32:2–19; Isaiah 36:2–22

Isaiah had warned Hezekiah not to join the uprising against Assyria (Isaiah 31:1), but the king had ignored the advice.

Knowing what had happened to Hoshea in Israel before this time would have made Hezekiah fearful when Assyria moved against him. So to keep them at bay Hezekiah offered tribute to Sennacherib hoping that the Assyrian army would not come up and attack Jerusalem (2 Kings 18:14–16). This tribute was gathered from the great Temple of Solomon in Jerusalem which was stripped of its treasures and sent off to appease the mighty conqueror.

Sennacherib surveyed what had been sent to him (2 Kings 18:14–16), and thought that Hezekiah had been stingy; surely Jerusalem must contain great treasure if he could send that quality and amount? So he became greedy, reasoning that Hezekiah would not have put everything in, and prepared to lay siege to Jerusalem.

READY OR NOT, HERE I COME

It was from his base camp at Lachish that Sennacherib turned his attention to Jerusalem, but he did not attack it in person, for he had huge resources at his disposal and was able to send a sizable portion of his army entrusting its success to others. The Assyrian administration was made up of three of his most senior officers, the supreme commander, his chief officer and his field commander.

- *Supreme commander was the TARTAN*, most likely a commander-in-chief or the field marshal of the Assyrian troops, some think it may have been Sennacherib's brother Sin-ah-usher who accompanied him on many operations.

- *Chief officer was the RABSARIS*, almost certainly the chief eunuch, whose duty would have been to act as Sennacherib's official scribe.

- *Field commander was the RABSHAKEH*, probably the second in command of the army. He was the one selected to speak for Sennacherib, possibly because he was fluent in Hebrew. Some have suggested that this was Sennacherib's prime minister. Could he have been an earlier Daniel, someone who was a first or second- generation Hebrew removed from Israel by previous Assyrian kings and trained up to serve his new masters? But unlike Daniel he gave himself over to the overthrow and not the maintenance of the Jewish people. Whoever he was, he was certainly gifted in both language and diplomatic skill.

The duty of these three was to intimidate Hezekiah into full surrender or to provoke such unrest within the citizens of Jerusalem that they would revolt and overthrow Hezekiah and receive grudgingly the yoke of Assyria. So this section of the army moved off to take the capital city of Judah, Jerusalem.

TUNNEL VISION

Notwithstanding his previous illness, Hezekiah, not knowing precisely when the invader would appear, had energetically and sensibly taken precautions so as not to be caught out.

Wisely he consulted others to see what preparations to make to withstand the coming onslaught (2 Chronicles 32:3–4). A major concern was ensuring that the Hebrews and not the Assyrians had access to the precious water supply (Isaiah 22:9–11). As the siege at Lachish took place during the summer of 701 BC, this was an important tactical move by Hezekiah. Jerusalem was in a very elevated location (Psalm 122), and relied on fresh water from springs and cisterns dug into the rock. These were suitably lined to collect rainwater for its population (Jeremiah 2:13). An invading army would have to ensure that a supply of fresh water was transported to its troops for if none was located in or around Jerusalem, their presence could not be maintained for long periods of time, especially in the great heat at that time of year.

Later in 2 Chronicles 32:30 it is recorded that Hezekiah also 'blocked the upper outlet of the Gihon spring and channelled the water down to the west side of the City of David' (see also 2 Kings 20:20).

LOOK WHAT I HAVE FOUND!

In 1880 a boy went into a tunnel that fed a pool called by the locals 'the Pool of Siloam' (but probably not the one referred to in John 9). That boy discovered writing scratched onto the wall in old Hebrew from before the exile in Babylon. The six-line inscription described how two gangs of workmen had started work at opposite ends and eventually broke through to meet up far underground in a marvellous feat of engineering skill. The Hebrew script points to a date contemporaneous with Hezekiah, and in all probability it comes from the time when Sennacherib set out to conqueror Judah.

The inscription is now in the antiquities museum in Istanbul, Turkey.

Hezekiah had strengthened the city to ensure that Jerusalem could hold out while awaiting help from Egypt to materialise. Excavators have also discovered the remains of a seven-metre-thick wall and tower that Hezekiah had constructed to withstand the Assyrian battering rams (2 Chronicles 32:5).

WAS IT LIKE THIS?

On Boxing Day (26 December) 2004, an abnormal calm descended on the coastline around the Indian Ocean. The sea had receded to an unusual extent, and many people had wandered out to view newly stranded fish, suddenly bereft of their natural environment. Also, unrealised wrecks and debris distracted the attention from the very real danger that many had exposed themselves too. The dark and ominous change to the horizon was noted by relatively few people, and the unwary were caught out with the rapid advance of the furious tsunami that rushed in and swept many away.

Likewise, Jerusalem waited in the sun, its preparations almost complete. Then horror struck its inhabitants as they viewed the dust cloud of this great host as it came up over the Judean hills towards them. In all probability lookout posts had been positioned on top of the great Temple of Solomon, and for a greater perspective, on the summit of the Mount of Olives. From that vantage point everything would have been in view, from the Dead Sea and the land of Moab in the east, towards Samaria in the north, and down over the Judean countryside to the south west.

The cry would have gone up, 'Here they come,' and the gates were bolted and barred for the long-dreaded evil day had arrived.

It has been estimated that the city covered 125 acres, and the population was about 25,000 people, which is small when compared to the 120,000 people living at Nineveh in the time of Jonah the prophet (Jonah 4:11), and Nineveh had expanded since that time.

Sennacherib's armies would have been full of blood lust having already conquered many of Judah's fortified cities. Many of Jerusalem's citizens, having received reports of their brutal activities, would have crowded the city walls to see the invaders for themselves.

Imagine then that you are the king of Judah, and you must decide what to do with the massive Assyrian army outside your gates. The warnings of Sennacherib as stated by his representative were no mere idle threats, for they were backed up by a huge show of force, with the promise of many reinforcements to come, if required.

TALK ABOUT A PANIC ATTACK!

The account of Sennacherib's siege of Jerusalem in the time of Hezekiah in the Bible is a brilliant piece of military reporting. It reveals how negotiations took place before any action commenced, for if a city or town could be persuaded to surrender then it made economic sense to negotiate a settlement.

The Assyrian representatives stopped at the aqueduct of the

Upper Pool on the road to the Washerman's field (2 Kings 18:17). Significantly this was the very place where Isaiah had called on Ahaz, Hezekiah's father, to trust the Lord and not Assyria (2 Kings 16:5–10; Isaiah 7:1–17).

Previously, Ahaz (king of Judah 732–716 BC), when threatened by a coalition of Israel and Syria, had in desperation turned to Assyria for help. The king who responded to his plea was Tiglath-Pileser III. Under that king's influence Ahaz corrupted the worship of the Lord by copying an impressive altar that he had seen in Syria (2 Kings 16:10–12). Knowing that they had succumbed to pagan influence in the past may have been a leverage that Rabshakeh would try to apply around the negotiating table.

Maybe this delegation had heard about Isaiah's words and in a deliberately provocative move stopped at the aqueduct, the very place he had spoken the word of the Lord.

When they arrived at the negotiation table they sat and waited for the Hebrew king to come to them, calling for him to appear before them. As Sennacherib had not materialised nor would Hezekiah, and as the Assyrian had sent three to negotiate so did Hezekiah, a macabre game was being played out with political niceties being observed.

The enemy of God's people (the devil) is always trying to look for weak links, and a particularly favourite strategy is to bring to remembrance past failures; the conscience needs to be cleansed so that he cannot succeed (Hebrews 9:14).

Sennacherib had carefully chosen those who would go to Jerusalem; he must have been confident that Lachish would not need their expertise. Likewise, Hezekiah carefully chose those whom he sent to parley on his behalf.

- *Eliakim son of Hilkiah* was the palace administrator.
- *Shebna* was the secretary, maybe the prime minister? But he had been demoted from palace administrator (compare Isaiah 22:15 with 36:3).
- *Joah son of Asaph* the recorder, whose job it was to faithfully record all the deliberations around the negotiating table.

SIX PROPOSITIONS FOR YOU TO PONDER

The one-sided negotiations were a cunning mixture of deception and psychological warfare by the Assyrians (2 Kings 18:19–27) so as to leave Hezekiah's representatives in no doubt about the precariousness of their position.

The Assyrians had a penchant for precision and the six propositions were divided into two groups, 1, 3 and 5 were practical (P) reasons and 2, 4, and 6 were theological (T) reasons for the Hebrews to capitulate.

1. (P) WOUNDS TO THE HAND (2 KINGS 18:19–21)

An appeal to reason formed the opening gambit. 'What foundation lies beneath your confidence?' the field commander asked. Hezekiah's ability as a commander and the resources at his disposal were also called into question. The echoing of Isaiah's warning about the reliability of Egypt was accompanied by a brilliant illustration of the precarious nature of its king and people: 'that splintered reed of a staff, which pierces a man's hand and wounds him if he leans on it!' (2 Kings 18:21).

2. (T) HEZEKIAH THE DESTROYER OF RELIGION (2 KINGS 18:22)

The attack then gets personal, for this man had intelligence about Hezekiah's reforms but deliberately twisted it to his own ends. He accused the king of removing God's altars on the high places, when he would have known full well that it was the Asherah poles and other items of idolatry that had been dismantled. He was trying to split the opposition for some may have been less than pleased with Hezekiah's actions.

Satan always seeks to distort the word of God and drive a wedge between God's people. If he can get others to do it as well, his purpose has been fulfilled. In the Garden of Eden, Eve then Adam succumbed to his evil reasoning. In the New Testament we see Jesus answering falsehood by always going back to the Scriptures and saying, 'It is written', a lesson worth noting and emulating (Matthew 4:1–11).

3. (P) SIZE DOES MATTER (2 KINGS 18:23–24)

Sennacherib thought he would intimidate Judah into surrendering (Isaiah 36:9). The Assyrians had more troops, greater military success, unparalleled domination of the world and, according to Sennacherib's thinking, they had to be right to win. He could not understand how Hezekiah dared refuse the invitation, for he had shown weakness in giving tribute to Sennacherib, and once weakness was exposed he was ready to exploit it and expected more compromises. An offer of two thousand horses for Hebrew cavalry to ride is a veiled insult. Hezekiah refuses to be drawn in and stands steadfast; he would not be intimidated by the numbers game.

4. (T) A FALSE PROPHETIC WORD (2 KINGS 18:25–30)

The abuse of prophecy was the next strand in his argument, for did they not understand that God himself had sent them to take

Jerusalem captive? Distortion of the word of God is often accompanied by lies; the New Testament warns against those who 'peddle the word of God for profit' (2 Corinthians 2:17).

STAND UP AND BE NOTICED

Up to this point the Assyrian delegates had been seated speaking to Hezekiah's representatives, but that all changed for now the commander *stood up* (2 Kings 18:28; Isaiah 36:13). This is a significant move in the negotiations. He was determined that the citizens of Jerusalem could not only clearly see him but also hear what he had to say.

The lingua franca (diplomatic speech) of that time was Akkadian, which was the most popular of a number of languages that were written in the cuneiform script (just as today many languages, for example English, French, Portuguese and Spanish, are written in the Roman script.) It was Akkadian that Paul used as an example of speaking in tongues in 1 Corinthians 14:20–22.

Dr Irvine Finkel of the British Museum has said that the language of the ancient Assyrians and Babylonians was 'harsh and brutal'.

Aramaic was developing as the lingua franca and would eventually replace Akkadian and then would be superseded by Greek after the conquests of Alexander the Great. Aramaic at that time was used diplomatically, particularly in the area covered by Israel and Judah, and a request was made for this tongue to be spoken in the ongoing negotiations (2 Kings 18:26), an appeal that was turned down because the residents of Jerusalem were to be under no illusions that their leaders would be able to save them. Diplomatic niceties were now replaced with brutal frankness and the commanders' words were laced with dire threats.

5. (P) WE PROMISE YOU PARADISE (2 KINGS 18:31–32)

Seeing that there was no response to his request, the field commander now gets abusive by attacking the leader who was steadfastly following God.

After the stick comes the carrot. Instead of living in this squalid little place you will be given more than you can imagine—vines, fig trees, water and then a bright future. In Egypt your God had promised you a land flowing with milk and honey (Exodus 3:8), but look where you are, up here in the Judean wilderness. My master will lead you into the true land that was promised.

How tempting this must have appeared! Did a few mouths start salivating at the thought of such fare? It was all so alluring.

6. (T) LOOK AROUND YOU (2 KINGS 18:33–35)

But nothing happened, no movement on the city walls, no white flag of surrender was hoisted above the battlements. So the Assyrian gets nasty and his scorn is tangible: how long do you think you can remain in your position, for sooner or later you will be forced to admit you have to surrender.

The gods of many nations are invoked to reinforce his arguments.

STAND FIRM

It would have been difficult to maintain a dignified inertia in the face of such threats; the temptation to panic must have been almost irresistible. But 'the people remained silent and said nothing in reply, because the king had commanded, "Do not answer him," ' (2 Kings 18:36).

The artificial words of Sennacherib's official offered a false security, for if Judah had accepted the Assyrians' invitation to meet him on common ground, the nation and not just Jerusalem would have been destroyed!

The Apostle Paul said about the Old Testament: 'These things happened to them as examples and were written down as warnings for us, on whom the fulfillment of the ages has come' (1 Corinthians 10:11). Sennacherib's attack against Jerusalem fits into the overall message of the Bible that God is fulfilling his plan of salvation in time and space for his people. Even though overwhelming odds are stacked against the church, believers have God on their side, and will ultimately triumph (1 John 4:4).

C. S. Lewis wisely wrote: 'To be always looking at the map when there is a fine prospect before you shatters the "wise passiveness" in which landscape ought to be enjoyed.'[1] An overview of the Bible ought similarly to be enjoyed, for God's outworking of redemption is revealed as a great panorama and not as a series of snapshots.

FOR FURTHER STUDY

1. In the wilderness Jesus was confronted by his enemy. Read of the tactics that Satan employed in Matthew 4:1–11 and what Jesus did and said to defeat him.
2. Flavius Josephus, in his Antiquities of the Jews, *Book 10, chapter 1, gives an interesting account of the events we have just looked at. It is*

worth obtaining it from the local lending library, or purchasing a copy to see what he says about the Assyrian siege of Jerusalem, and many other things recorded in the Bible.

3. Read Ephesians 6:10–20 to see what Paul says about being adequately protected against the Christian's enemy.

TO THINK ABOUT AND DISCUSS

1. Christians who are persecuted for their faith, either mentally or physically, must be tempted to compromise or give in so that they can live a peaceful life. Would you think it cowardice or common sense to take the pragmatic view?

2. In 2 Corinthians 10:4–5, Paul speaks about Christian warfare. What does he mean and how should these weapons be used?

3. Can you think of ways that you can help others who are struggling in their lives to maintain a good Christian witness?

4. How best can believers be supported who live under regimes that openly persecute Christians?

5. How can the plan of God be seen and understood in other passages from the Old Testament?

Note

1 **C. S. Lewis,** The Discarded Image: An introduction to medieval and renaissance literature (Cambridge University Press), page ix.

4 Who is God?

2 Kings 19:1–34; 2 Chronicles 32:20; Isaiah 37:1–35

Jerusalem was in a desperate situation, despite Hezekiah's plans and preparation. It seems that the sheer size of the Assyrian army sent against it was larger than anything Hezekiah could have imagined in his worst nightmares.

CHALLENGE THROWN DOWN

In the time of Elijah the prophet, the issue of 'who is God?' had to be faced in a confrontation with the prophets of Baal on Mount Carmel. The false god Baal was worshipped by the Hittites and many other nations around and beyond the Mediterranean basin, and when Jezebel set him up in Israel, the prophet Elijah took him on. Baal was the god of storm, often depicted with a thunder club in right hand and lightning fork in left. This makes it all the more significant that he was defeated by fire at the contest on Mount Carmel, on a clear day, as 1 Kings 18 records. Also Elijah was taken up into heaven in a whirlwind, through the air, which many thought to be under the control of Baal.

In the New Testament Jesus is accused of being under the influence of Beelzebub (one variation of Baal), the god of flies and dung. In response Jesus said that he was not of the devil, and whoever said he was would be guilty of the blasphemy against the Holy Spirit (Mark 3:20–30).

DIFFERENT GODS SAME PROBLEM

The Assyrians were no different to the nations around them and religious rituals and practices were part of their daily rhythms.

Their main deity was Asher, the god of the Assyrian nation. It was said to be solely in his power to grant (or remove) kingship over Assyria, and the Assyrian king was his chief priest and representative on earth. This god supported and encouraged the armies and conquests were achieved in his name and for his glory.

Another of their deities was Inana (also known as Ishtar), the goddess of love and war (probably more accurate to say, sex and violence). The planet Venus was connected with her. Her symbol was the eight-pointed star and her sacred ceremonial animal was the lion.[1]

Lions have always attracted attention; their majesty, colour, manes and power all lead to kingly comparisons. It was an eminently suitable emblem for Nineveh's power and might. Sennacherib the Lion was a formidable monarch and thought that he could subdue any nation and whatever deity it honoured. The question was asked outside Jerusalem's walls by his representative, 'How can the Lord deliver Jerusalem from my hand?' Like many others he thought that Israel's God was dead, or, if alive, he was powerless to intervene for good— but that was Sennacherib's terrible mistake.

Isaiah had previously spoken against arrogant opposition and its true nature: 'No longer will the fool be called noble nor the scoundrel be highly respected. For the fool speaks folly, his mind is busy with evil: He practises ungodliness and spreads error concerning the LORD; the hungry he leaves empty and from the thirsty he withholds water' (Isaiah 32:5–6).

The opposition of Sennacherib presents the pattern of all who oppose God's rule for their lives. The root of opposition to God is lawlessness (1 John 3:4), and the Assyrian aggression is shown up as sinful when compared to the Law of God.

TEN COMMANDMENTS FOR ALL

Sennacherib ridiculed those who trusted in God and followed the Lord's commandments (Isaiah 36:7). But he was the one in error, for the commands of God are not just for the Jewish people but also for everyone in every time and place.

It is sad to see how the Ten Commandments in particular were challenged by the might of Assyria and her representatives, for in their words and actions all rebellion against God is reflected.

1. YOU SHALL HAVE NO OTHER GODS BEFORE ME

'Your god is not better than any other outside of Assyria, and they have all fallen before the might of my master.' From the pagan perspective, Sennacherib thought that Hezekiah's destruction of the high places and insistence on worship only in the Temple (2 Kings 18:22; 2 Chronicles 29:21–35; 30:15–24; 31:3) would anger God. Such a concentration of worship to one location was unknown in the heathen world. Sennacherib's envoys sneered at Hezekiah's faith and insinuated that the king's actions of restoration would provoke God's punishment.

Sennacherib decided what God wanted and then proceeded to offer that kind of worship, totally unconcerned about God's will. However, Sennacherib's ignorance proved to be fatally flawed, for God's commands applied to him and his people as well as to the Israelites.

2. YOU SHALL NOT MAKE AN IDOL FOR YOURSELF

An idol can be in any form, not just stone statues or possessions, but ideas and concepts. The Assyrians had made their gods and the power of their invincible army and way of life into idols.

Today many who spurn the Christian way make idols out of various things: their hobbies, sport, pop music, possessions, money, health, but they can never and must never replace the one true God.

3. YOU SHALL NOT MISUSE THE NAME OF THE LORD YOUR GOD

In a cunning display of verbal dexterity the Lord had been discredited and his name defamed by the Rabshakeh. In many places today the name of Jesus is used in a wrong way. Yet none stop to think why is it that when things go wrong, it is not Allah, Amun, Buddha or Kali that is uttered in frustration or pain, but Jesus, or Jesus Christ. The devil will only attack and pull down the truth, for why should he bother to put down lies?

4. REMEMBER THE SABBATH DAY BY KEEPING IT HOLY

If the Rabshakeh was a first or second-generation Hebrew, he would know how important the Sabbath was to them. So in trying to remove the people of Judah he would also have had a detrimental effect on their devotion to God.

Today many Christians do the devil's work for him by not thinking about the Lord's Day, what it is for and how it should be used.

5. HONOUR YOUR FATHER AND MOTHER

If the Rabshakeh's words could penetrate to a weak link, then he might succeed in driving a wedge between families. Hezekiah had given the order as their ruling father not to respond, and Isaiah as their spiritual father would speak the Lord's word to them. But it is not too great a stretch of the imagination to see how the feeble or headstrong might go against the wishes of their parents and betray the cause of God. Divided families are a curse and not a blessing. Rabshakeh would have clearly understood that and would have sought to exploit it to the determent of all the inhabitants of the city.

6. YOU SHALL NOT MURDER

There may well have been Hebrews caught in earlier conflicts that were killed by impalement or some other ghastly means to drive home the Assyrians' point. Yet the right-thinking person would have concluded from the dying, 'what would prevent them from killing us also in future if we surrendered?' The sanctity of life is often abused when God does not have his rightful place in the life of a nation.

7. YOU SHALL NOT COMMIT ADULTERY

All adultery is firstly against God (Ezekiel 23), and this Assyrian official was trying to get the people to prostitute themselves by following after other gods. A sad by-product, if they capitulated, would have been exposure to false teaching and moral behaviour which would have been detrimental to many.

8. YOU SHALL NOT STEAL

The Assyrians were aiming to take that which was not theirs. Might is not right, and just because they were bullies it did not give them licence to take away another's city, people and possessions.

9. YOU SHALL NOT GIVE FALSE TESTIMONY

Previously Hezekiah had been told that if tribute were paid then the Assyrian army would leave Judah, but as soon as Hezekiah paid the tribute, Sennacherib launched a siege on Jerusalem (2 Kings 18:17). So now why should Hezekiah and the Hebrews believe what Sennacherib told them? He could just as easily change his mind again. As Sennacherib's representative, Rabshakeh was without integrity for he had no concern or sensitivity for anyone except his master (Isaiah 36:8).

10. YOU SHALL NOT COVET

The Hebrews had been led by God out of bondage in Egypt into a land flowing with milk and honey (Exodus 3:8). They were also to be the priestly and holy nation (Exodus 19:6), not hoarding but dispensing the knowledge of God throughout the whole earth.

To achieve this God had placed them at the crossroads of the world, the land link from Europe to Asia and Africa, and such a rich and vital place attracted the attention of others, so the Assyrians coveted what was not theirs by rights.

THE LAW HAS TEETH

Sennacherib was going to be revealed not as the all-powerful conqueror but as a man who had to submit to the true King of the universe, a lesson that many learn, often when it is too late for them to repent of their sins. All who go against God's law will be judged by that law unless someone stands in their place and takes full responsibility for their sinful actions.

The New Testament reveals that the Lord Jesus Christ alone is the one who not only bears the sin of his people but who is also the only way to God (John 14:6; 1 Timothy 2:5–6).

WHY DO CHRISTIANS SUFFER?

This persecution of Hezekiah, Isaiah and the people of Judah seems unfair to many. Why, if we are the people of God, does he allow us to go through trials? This is a question that countless others have asked, when in varying circumstances they seemed to have been singled out for pain and anguish.

The apostle Paul deals with it in Colossians 1:24, 'Now I rejoice in what was suffered for you, and I fill up in my flesh what is still lacking in regard to Christ's afflictions, for the sake of his body, which is the church.'

When he wrote I 'suffered for you' he meant for the church, for the service of Jesus Christ is always costly. But he also suffered as an example to the persecuted church; they were not alone, isolated from the rest of the body of Christ, and he was able to empathise with them in their situation.

So it was with Hezekiah and the people in Jerusalem; they could sympathise with their fellow countrymen and then be a greater blessing to Judah in future.

YOU ARE NOT INDISPENSABLE

The experience of suffering and persecution made Paul a better person, not because he was proud of his sufferings but because he used them to prove that God cared for and loved him.

It was also a means for releasing others for service, a hard lesson to learn for such an energetic man, for if he were sidelined then others would need to get involved. The work of the church is individuals working together as a collective whole, so with the great Isaiah holed up with no apparent means of escape, who would fulfil his role in Judah? We are not given any names but God always has his servants, the known and the unknown who work for him, whatever the situation. This was a hard lesson that Elijah also had to learn (1 Kings 19:18). It is also a lesson that many Christians would do well to learn.

FOR FURTHER STUDY

1. Read in 1 Kings 8 to discover the astonishing events that happened when Solomon's Temple was dedicated.
2. Now read the extraordinary claims of Paul about the new temple that God is constructing in 1 Corinthians 3:16–17.
3. Suffering is spoken of in many places in the Bible; read John 15:18–21 and list all the things that Jesus says about persecution and the reasons for it taking place.

TO THINK ABOUT AND DISCUSS

1. How should the third commandment recorded in Exodus 20:7 and Deuteronomy 5:11 impact people's lives today?

2. If you are suffering for the Christian faith, what comfort, if any, can you derive from the fact that others are also suffering for the sake of Christ?

3. If you are not suffering for being a Christian at present, it does not mean that in future you will not be spared these things. What steps are you now taking so that in future your faith is not rocked by persecution?

4. Do you think that you are indispensable to your church and that its work and witness depends on you? How difficult is it to come to terms with the fact that God may well choose others to do something that you think only you can do?

Note

1   **Clive Anderson,** *Opening Up Nahum* (Leominster: Day One, 2005), p. 74.

5 Like a bird in a cage

2 Kings 19:1–34; 2 Chronicles 32:20; Isaiah 37:1–35

Christians generally view the dramatic events in these passages through the lens of the Old Testament. Historians by and large look at them through the monuments and inscriptions that have survived. But the Christian historian uses both the Bible and the archaeological remains to build up the fullest picture possible, for they give an unparalleled opportunity to look at the event from both sides, Assyrian as well as Hebrew.

COLONEL TAYLOR'S DISCOVERY

In 1830 Colonel R. Taylor, the British representative in Baghdad, discovered among the ruins of ancient Nineveh a six-sided hexagonal clay prism that is now known as the Taylor Prism. Inscribed on it is Sennacherib's own description of his campaign of 701 BC, including his siege of Jerusalem in the time of Hezekiah. It is well worth reading:

As for Hezekiah the Judahite, who did not submit to my yoke: forty-six of his strong, walled cities, as well as the small towns in their area, which were without number, by levelling with battering-rams and by bringing up siege-engines, and by attacking and storming on foot, by mines, tunnels and breeches, I besieged and took them. 200,150 people, great and small, male and female, horses, mules, asses, camels, cattle and sheep without number, I brought away from them and counted as spoil. [Hezekiah] himself, like a caged bird I shut up in Jerusalem, his royal city. I threw up earthworks against him—the one coming out of the city-gate, I turned back to his misery. His cities, which I had despoiled, I cut off from his land, and to Mitinti, king of Ashdod, Padi, king of Ekron, and Silli-bêl, king of Gaza, I gave (them). And thus I diminished his land. I added to the former tribute, and I laid upon him the surrender of their land and imposts—gifts for my majesty. As for Hezekiah, the terrifying splendour of my majesty overcame him, and the Arabs and his mercenary troops which he had brought in to strengthen Jerusalem, his royal city, deserted him. In addition to the thirty talents of gold and eight hundred talents of silver, gems, antimony, jewels, large carnelians, ivory-inlaid couches, ivory-inlaid chairs, elephant hides, elephant tusks, ebony, boxwood, all kinds of valuable treasures, as well as his daughters, his harem, his male and female musicians, which he had brought after me to Nineveh, my royal city. To pay tribute and to accept servitude, he dispatched his messengers.

Some of the tribute paid is referred to above as 'thirty talents of gold and eight hundred talents of silver', whereas the 2 Kings 18:14 records 'three hundred talents of silver and thirty talents of gold'. These two accounts seem irreconcilable but more recent discoveries have revealed that, although the method of calculating the weight of gold was the same for both Judah and Assyria, that for weighing silver was very different. It took exactly 800 Assyrian talents of silver to equal 300 Judean talents!

Sennacherib's recording of this event ends abruptly, which

raises suspicion that his scribes had concealed something. For although Sennacherib recorded that he shut up Hezekiah in his royal city 'like a caged bird', his problem was that he did not have the key to unlock the door to get in and remove the troublesome king from his throne.

GOD'S RECORD AND GOD'S MAN

So what of the Bible and its record of these things? The principal character in what happened next is God himself, and his word spoken through his prophet into this hopeless situation.

The three men that Hezekiah had sent to negotiate returned with bad tidings and in response he did two things and heard two things.

Firstly, Hezekiah tore his clothes and covered himself in sackcloth, customary signs of mourning, and then in his helplessness he sent a delegation to Isaiah the prophet. He also heard unbelief had been expressed in the words of those men when they said, 'It may be that the LORD *your* God heard all the words of [Rabshakeh]' (2 Kings 19:4; Isaiah 37:4, my italics). Were they sceptical or afraid that their God was not up to facing down the Assyrians? Previously Isaiah had spoken a prophetic word about Shebna and Eliakim, unfaltering to one and elevating to the other, but now looking at the Assyrian army camped outside the city wall were they full of doubt as to the accuracy of Isaiah's predictions and subsequent fulfilment? (Isaiah 22:15–24).

Hezekiah also heard from Isaiah, and what a message of hope it was, full of expectation about the withdrawal of the Assyrians and that on their return Sennacherib would die by the sword (2 Kings 19:6–7; Isaiah 37:6). This record is in the Bible, which is called the sword of the Spirit (Ephesians 6:17).

BURSTING THE BALLOON OF ASSYRIAN POMPOSITY

Immediately after Hezekiah had sought the godly prophet, the proud Rabshakeh had to leave to return and help his master at Libnah (2 Kings 19:8–9; Isaiah 37:8–9). Egypt had been described as 'that splintered reed of a staff, which pierces a man's hand and wounds him if he leans on it!' (2 Kings 18:21). But it was the inflated ego of the Assyrian that was in danger of being punctured, and so Rabshakeh and no doubt a substantial escort left to help out a potentially dangerous situation.

The assault on Libnah was proceeding and Taharqa (crown prince but future Pharaoh) came to take on the Assyrians. Maybe Hezekiah thought that God would honour the alliance that he had made with Egypt and use them to thrust out the Assyrians from his land, but Isaiah's warnings were not vain words (Isaiah 18:1–4, 30:1–8, and 31:1–3).

According to the Assyrian annals, Sennacherib boasted:

In the plain of Altaqua, their ranks were drawn up before me, they sharpened their weapons. Upon a trust oracle given by Ashur, my Lord, I fought with them and brought about their defeat. The Egyptian charioteers and princes, together with the charioteers of the Kushite king, my hands took alive in the midst of the battle.

This battle took place about half way between Ashdod and Joppa, and the Assyrians were victorious, sending Taharqa scurrying back to Egypt. So it was that Hezekiah had a great shock, for Rabshakeh returned, not in person but in words brought by a messenger. Previously Hezekiah had reasoned that with the removal of his illness: 'Will there not be peace and security in my lifetime?' (2 Kings 20:19). It was a hard lesson to learn that God does not work to our agenda, nor is he obliged to fulfil our fantasies.

SPREAD IT OUT

Sin is an ogre which drives all beautiful things into hiding. But instead of disappearing so that he could not be found and leaving his people to fend for themselves, Hezekiah, on receiving details of the Assyrians' demands, approached the throne of God in prayer. For this godly man realised that he could not win using the power of his army alone, and as king he was obliged to remain with his people come what may.

The power of prayer comes through in these Bible passages and all Christian believers should be challenged and motivated to pray because of Hezekiah's action and God's reaction. Hezekiah remembered Solomon's great prayers at the dedication of the Temple and that all of God's children were to understand the need to follow in his ways (1 Kings 8:30; 2 Chronicles 7:14).

A PATTERN PRAYER

Hezekiah approached God in a set way, and the formula he used is a good one to learn and employ in times of prayer and need.

1. HEZEKIAH SPREAD OUT HIS REQUEST (2 KINGS 19:14; ISAIAH 37:14)

It often helps to focus the mind to have a prayer diary, or to show God the problem that needs dealing with by writing out a specific predicament.

2 Chronicles 32:17 shows that Sennacherib bombarded Hezekiah with letters, each one designed to erode his resolve and to bring him to his knees. Many Christians often feel overwhelmed by problems; in such situations it is best to tell God about them.

2. HEZEKIAH ACKNOWLEDGES GOD'S SUPREMACY (2 KINGS 19:15; ISAIAH 37:16)

Never forget that the one who is enthroned in heaven is the Lord of all and must be approached in a right and reverent way.

3. HEZEKIAH PARTICULARISED THE PROBLEM (2 KINGS 19:16; ISAIAH 37:17)

Almighty God is a person and can be approached, so do not be afraid to tell him all about your needs.

4. HEZEKIAH FACED UP TO HIS FEARS (2 KINGS 19:17–18; ISAIAH 37:18–19)

How difficult it is to admit helplessness in the face of trouble, but Hezekiah overcame his fears and clearly stated them.

5. HEZEKIAH HUMBLY MADE A SPECIFIC REQUEST (2 KINGS 19:19; ISAIAH 37:20)

Shyness or the feeling of inadequacy often prevents many from being specific in prayer. Instead of prevaricating around the bush, God delights to hear particular needs and appeals for help; directness should not be shunned but practised.

A PROPHETIC RESPONSE

Moved by the Spirit of God (2 Peter 1:21), Isaiah responded to

Hezekiah's prayer, the reply also had a number of component parts.

1. JERUSALEM WOULD NOT BE VIOLATED (2 KINGS 19:21; ISAIAH 37:22)

This great oppressive army may have raped and pillaged across the land, but they would not penetrate Zion who in contempt would toss her head at them as a mark of disdain.

2. THE OFFENDED PARTY IS IDENTIFIED (2 KINGS 19:22–24; ISAIAH 37:23–25)

Assyria had not insulted a mere idol or false god but the Holy One of Israel, and had bitten off far more than she could chew. Assyria's claims were miniscule compared to the omnipotence of God.

3. AN APPEAL IS MADE TO HISTORY AND MODERNITY (2 KINGS 19:25–27; ISAIAH 37:26–28)

Has it been forgotten how God brought this small nation out of bondage in Egypt and into this land? Remember the past victories he had wrought for the Hebrews. The Assyrians were treading on dangerous ground and they would realise that God is not impotent. For he knew exactly where they were, and that knowledge was turned into power for he would strike more precisely then any laser-guided missile.

4. A JUDGEMENT IS PRONOUNCED (2 KINGS 19:28; ISAIAH 37:29)

Many Assyrian inscriptions show captives being led away with hooks through their noses, a sign of subjection and control, but the measure they used would now be used on them (Matthew 7:2).

5. HEZEKIAH WILL BENEFIT BY YOUR DEMISE (2 KINGS 19:30–32; ISAIAH 37:30–32)

Sennacherib was clearly told that the crops would grow and the harvest would be gathered in, so he wouldn't have opportunity to salt the land to destroy its fertility, nor would he be present to stop this process. These words may have seemed fanciful to all concerned, but see what happened, for God was at work.

6. ASSYRIA WILL NOT ASSAULT JERUSALEM (2 KINGS 19:32–34; ISAIAH 37:33–35)

The first encounter with the Assyrians was limited and earth works and siege ramps had not been constructed. Maybe they were just commencing these when the order came to go to Libnah and help out the main Assyrian force when it was realised that Egypt was on the move. They hoped to trap Egypt in a pincher movement.

7. THE WORD OF GOD WAS FULFILLED (2 KINGS 19:35; ISAIAH 37:36)

After dealing with Libnah and the Egyptian army, did the letters to Hezekiah contain the frightening words, 'we are now coming to get you?'

This prophetic word was probably written out and sent post haste to the Assyrians, for the fulfilment of Isaiah's words was rapid. Before they could respond, either in kind or with violence, the angel of the LORD fulfilled the word of the LORD (2 Kings 19:35).

JESUS AND SENNACHERIB

It may be a complete surprise to link these two kings, but they did meet in battle in 701 BC! For according to the Bible, Jesus had appeared on earth before he came as a baby to Bethlehem; these appearances are known as a theophany, meaning 'to show'.[1] In the Old Testament a distinction is made between an angel of the Lord and *the* angel of the Lord; *the* angel of the Lord is Jesus.

In his defence in Acts 7, Stephen the first Christian martyr takes his accusers on a tour of the Old Testament and says that the one who sent Moses 'was sent to be their ruler and deliverer by God himself through *the* angel who appeared to him in the bush' (v.35). Then more clearly, 'This is the Moses who told the Israelites, "God will send you a prophet like me from your own people." He was in the assembly in the desert, with *the* angel who spoke to him on Mount Sinai' (vv.37–38). That *the* angel is unmistakably God is evident in the Scriptures with the clearest clue being given in Genesis 31: '*the* angel of God said to me in a dream, "I am the God of Bethel," ' (v.13).

Can this really be Jesus? It is a salutary reminder that although the Lord Jesus can be known as 'gentle Jesus meek and mild', he is also the Lord of life, death and the afterlife (Revelation 1:18), and this Jesus performed a terrifying role in the destruction of the Assyrian forces.

Just as at the first Passover in Egypt, when 'the LORD struck down all the firstborn in Egypt' (Exodus 12:29), so here in Israel, '*the* angel of the LORD went out and put to death a hundred and eighty five thousand men in the Assyrian camp' (2 Kings 19:35). This had been prophesied by Isaiah and the word was fulfilled in every respect (Isaiah 31:8–9). How terrifying it must have been to Sennacherib to see the might of his all-conquering army lying still in death.

Lord Byron portrayed these events memorably:

For the Angel of Death spread his wings on the blast,
And breathed in the face of the foe as he passed;
And the eyes of the sleepers waxed deadly and chill,
And their hearts but once heaved, and for ever grew still!

The location of this event is not given, but it was possibly near Libnah, after the battle with the Egyptians, and intriguingly the mass grave of those who perished that night may one day be discovered. Herodotus the Greek historian tells of an Assyrian retreat due to rodent infestation (and subsequent plague?) while they were at Pelusium in northeast Egypt. Although this is in the wrong place for this event, it is of interest to see what he wrote:

Thousands of field-mice swarmed over them during the night, and ate their quivers, their bowstrings, and the leather handles of their shields, so that the following day, having no arms to fight with, they abandoned their position and suffered severe losses during their retreat.[2]

Sennacherib returned to his capital at Nineveh, but these things were not recorded. It was the destruction of Lachish that adorned the walls of his victory room and the only mention of Jerusalem was in various inscriptions. One scholar does, however, think that Jerusalem may be depicted on a damaged relief from Sennacherib's throne hall, with no inscription describing the city in view.[3]

On the Lachish relief a camp is depicted at the end of the

sequence of events. Could it be Sennacherib, trying to show that his camp was at peace, and whatever had taken place was edited out from all the Assyrian records?

VICTORY GOES TO THE STRONGEST

The prayers of the righteous were triumphant (2 Kings 19:20). Assyria's confidence in her manufactured gods was betrayed because she had a false concept of Israel's God, who alone is Lord of the whole earth (Exodus 19:5). All the religious profession and practices of Assyria failed miserably, and it was brought about by a gross ignorance of religious knowledge (2 Kings 19:22–23).

This sorry state would continue for another eighty-nine years until, amid great carnage, Nineveh fell in August 612 BC. Her temples were filled with the slaughter of many penitents crying out for help to the deities they represented, but instead of relief, the houses of their gods became their tombs. It is a sad fact that many have perished down the centuries in places they have fled to for refuge.

False gods all pass away but the one true and eternal God will never be irrelevant or forgotten, for he lives for ever, and he will not give his glory to any other.

This page of Israel's history is one of the most inspiring, for here in this account, Hezekiah's faith can be seen as he led Judah to an absolute trust in God's protection through the ministry of Isaiah. His faith resulted in the complete humbling of the mighty Assyrian army, not by his own effort but through the power of God. The defeat of Sennacherib portrays the destiny awaiting all who are guided by selfishness and who oppose God's will.

Sennacherib survived this disaster a further twenty years; but he never again renewed his attempt to take Jerusalem.

SPIN DOCTORS AT WORK

Despite the Bible's account about Sennacherib suffering a heavy defeat, he was not slow to cast events in a very different light. The Assyrians rarely referred to defeat in battle and never to their casualties, for to record such things would weaken their prestige and influence but also make sorry reading for future generations who would be indoctrinated with their glorious past.

FOR FURTHER STUDY

1. How many other appearances of the Lord Jesus in the Old Testament can you find, and what is the significance of each appearing?

2. Proverbs 29:25 clearly speaks of right priorities for the believer. In how many other places in Proverbs can a similar sentiment be found?

TO THINK ABOUT AND DISCUSS

1. Sennacherib's inscriptions were a catalogue of boasting. How can a Christian respond when so many who are against God try to show that the church is weak and that Christians are relying on a false hope?

2. Is it a surprise that Jesus was the one who killed the Assyrians when the New Testament Gospels portray him as the resurrection and the life (John 11:25)? How can these two seemingly contradictory facts be reconciled?

3. *Revelation 20:11–15 portrays a frightening scene. Is that going to be fulfilled or is it just poetic language for something else?*

Notes

1 **Christoph Uehlinger,** 'Clio in a world of pictures', in **Lester L. Grabb,** ed., *Like a Bird in a Cage* (Sheffield: Sheffield Academic Press), p. 300.

2 See **Jonathan Stephen,** *Theophany: Close encounters with the Son of God* (Epsom: Day One, 1998), for an excellent treatment of this subject.

3 **Herodotus,** *The Histories* (Harmondsworth: Penguin Classics), pp. 185–186.

6 Return to Nineveh

2 Kings 19:36; 2 Chronicles 32:21; Isaiah 37:37

Bruised, bloodied but unbowed, Sennacherib returned home in disgrace (2 Chronicles 32:21b), but he did not die immediately because of his blasphemy and arrogance. He set about improving and enlarging his power base, with the probable secondary purpose of deflecting attention away from such an abject defeat. For by redirecting the thoughts of his people away from mourning their lost sons, they could glory in his great building works at Nineveh.

WHY SENNACHERIB CHOSE NINEVEH FOR HIS CAPITAL

Sennacherib's father Sargon II (Akkadian, *Sharru-Kenu*, 'legitimate king') was a son of (?) Tiglath-Pileser III (745–727 BC) and appears to have seized the throne from Shalmaneser V in a violent coup. Sargon's immediate concern had been dealing with resistance inside Assyria. This instability at the centre of the empire gave rise to a rebellion in Syria led by Yau-bi'di, king of Hamath. Sargon defeated this coalition and the skinning alive of Yau-bi'di was portrayed in detail on the walls of Sargon's palace in the new city of Dur-Sharrukin (modern Khorsabad) whose foundations were laid in 717 BC. However, in the south Sargon's forces were beaten in 720 BC by an army supporting the Babylonian king, Merodach-Baladan.

Sargon scarcely stopped fighting throughout his reign. A campaign in 714 BC weakened the powerful northern state of Urartu and the surviving report is in the form of a letter from Sargon to the god Ashur, a tablet now in the Louvre. In 710 BC he retook Babylonia, defeating Merodach-Baladan, and this great triumph was followed by the celebrations of the completion of the new city of Dur-Sharrukin ('Fortress of Sargon'), north of Nineveh. But in 705 BC a military emergency in Anatolia required the king's personal participation and Sargon was killed in battle.

Sennacherib thought that the gods must have been angry with his father, for not only had Sargon been killed on the field of battle, but his corpse had not been recovered. This was a serious matter for the ancient Assyrians, for a king's body required burial accompanied by the proper rituals at the holy city of Ashur. In an incomplete and difficult text referred to as 'The sin of Sargon', this event is mentioned, and Sennacherib makes a number of veiled illusions to it, but no official record is extant, because that would not put his or Sargon's reign in a good light for succeeding generations. However, Sennacherib does claim to have wrestled with the reasons for his father's god-forsaken death throughout his reign.

In response to this disaster, Sennacherib selected not the old capital city of Calah (Nimrud) but the ancient city of Nineveh for his capital, also rejecting Khorsabad, so that his father's misfortune would not transfer to him.

IS THIS NOT GREAT NINEVEH THAT I HAVE BUILT?

A particularly striking example of Sennacherib's creativity was his building of Nineveh in its final form. It was already ancient and famous, but Sennacherib planned and rebuilt it in a park-like setting which must have made it one of the fairest of ancient cities, as well as, in terms of extent, one of the greatest.

Prior to the invasion of Judah, Sennacherib had begun building projects at his capital city. From 700 BC, on his return home, building accelerated and the palaces' walls were constructed.

The site of Nineveh was on the east bank of the Tigris, where a minor tributary, the Khosr, joins the main river. Sennacherib enlarged the site and provided it with two walls for protection. The outer wall, made of great limestone blocks, was 'raised mountain high' while the inner wall had fifteen named major gates built with mud brick and stone. The eastern section of the wall was about three miles (five kilometres) long and contained six gates. The southern section was only half a mile long (eight hundred metres) and contained one gate, the western section was two and a half miles long (four kilometres) and contained five gates. The northern section of the wall was one and a half miles long (two and a half kilometres) and had three gates.

Most impressive was the Shamash gate, which was approached across two moats and a watercourse by a series of bridges. Its walls were faced with limestone and were surmounted with a crenulated parapet. The structure was built of mud and burnt bricks and bore the stamp of Sennacherib.

A classical author said that the walls of the city were wide enough for three chariots to be driven abreast on them, and this statement is confirmed by the extant remains, which are some twelve metres (forty feet) thick. A further line of defence was provided by a curving outer wall running well east of the city from the Tigris upstream to the Tigris downstream.

Nineveh was an early example of town planning, for within the inner walls there were new streets, enlarged squares and splendid buildings.

OFF TO THE PALACE

Sennacherib's principal building was a new palace, which he named 'palace without a rival', to replace a smaller, earlier one. Standing on a terrace high above an old riverbed, it covered an area of two and a half acres. In an inscription showing Sennacherib's willingness to accept new ideas, he wrote:

Beams of cedar, the product of mount Amanus, which they dragged with difficulty out of (these) distant mountains, I stretched across their roofs. Great door-leaves of cypress, whose odour is pleasant as they are opened and closed, I bound with a band of shining copper and set them up in their doors. A portico patterned after a Hittite palace, which they call in the Amorite tongue bit hilani, I constructed inside for my lordly pleasure.

The king would have supervised his building construction, and a number of carved wall panels show him in his chariot looking on as various items are prepared and put into place.

A FORERUNNER OF ISAMBARD KINGDOM BRUNEL?

Like an early Brunel, the great Victorian engineer, the king had an interest in technology and also claims to have invented new techniques in bronze-casting:

I, Sennacherib, through the acute intelligence which the noble god Ea had granted me and with my own experimenting, achieved the casting of bronze colossal lions which no king had done before me. Over great posts and palm trunks I built a clay mould for twelve colossal lions together with twelve enormous colossal bulls and poured bronze therein as in casting half-shekel pieces.

He also incorporated architectural features from Syrian buildings, and the palace was adorned internally with alabaster, ivory and ornamental and scented woods, and on the external walls with coloured glazed bricks. Did he use any of Hezekiah's tribute, 'three hundred talents of silver and thirty talents of gold … [which included gold stripped off the temple doors and doorposts] all the silver that was found in the temple of the LORD and in the treasuries of the royal palace' (2 Kings 18:14–16)? As a gesture of defiance he may well have done, and today, under the great mound of Kuyunjik, may still lie buried some of this treasure stripped from Solomon's great temple.

Many of the walls of Sennacherib's palace were decorated with triumphant scenes from foreign campaigns as well as those depicting the carving, transport and placing of colossal bull statues. The message of these reliefs was twofold. First, it was one of reassurance that foreign neighbours were under control and that the borders were secure. Secondly, they would serve as a warning to visiting dignitaries and envoys that Assyria would brook no interference in its foreign policy and that payment of tribute was to be maintained—if not, the consequences were staring them in the face.

In its prime, Sennacherib's palace must have been

magnificent. Certainly, to the indigenous inhabitants of the land, who lived mainly in simple mud-brick dwellings with a thatched roof, it must have appeared overwhelmingly opulent.

It was a great visual testimony to the power and supremacy of the Assyrians and the ordinary citizen would have rested assured that their king was able to protect them from any danger. How soon the debacle in Judah was forgotten can be gauged from the fact that in room thirty-six of his palace, Sennacherib adorned the walls with scenes from the successful campaign against Lachish. The God of the Hebrews was considered not as powerful as many thought, and Sennacherib thought he would prove it by omitting Jerusalem from the walls of his palace.

HIGHWAY ENGINEERING

For the approach to his palace Sennacherib built a road of limestone slabs twenty-seven metres (ninety feet) wide. To encroach on this road by private buildings was an offence punishable by impalement, a ghastly death and a forerunner of crucifixion. This was the manner of death that Haman had planned for Mordecai in Esther but eventually he was the one hoisted onto the stake (Esther 7:10). The New Testament links these two things together when it says of Jesus, 'they killed him by hanging him on a tree' (Acts 10:39), not by his neck but by crucifixion.

The possibility of encroachment shows that private building must have taken place in some parts of the city, although Sennacherib gives no details of this. Not forgetting the ordinary person, he does, however, state that upstream of the city he made plots of land available to citizens for planting orchards. This shows a political sensitivity towards his own people, something sadly lacking in his foreign policy.

HANGING GARDENS OF NINEVEH

To the side of his palace Sennacherib constructed 'a great park like unto mount Amanus, wherein were planted all kinds of herbs and fruit trees'.

It was probably built for his queen, Naqi'a-Zakutu, to help her remember her homeland and to make her feel more comfortable at the king's side.

Irrigation would be all important if this wonder of the world were not to shrivel and die. The Tigris ran alongside the city, but it was too low in its bed to be used for irrigation for much of the year, and in the summer the Khosr tributary diminished to a trickle. Sennacherib therefore carried out major engineering works to feed waters from mountain streams, up to fifty miles away, into the Khosr. An elaborate system of canals, aqueducts, weirs and sluices controlled the flow. A three-hundred-metre stretch of an aqueduct, containing about two million stone blocks of a quarter of a ton each, still exists, and remains of some of the weirs, and of brick-lined sections of the canals, are still to be seen. The water irrigated his great park, in which there were all kinds of scented plants and fruit trees, a welcome amenity in a great city. The run-off water was not wasted, but was fed into an area allowed to develop into a swamp, where there was encouragement of colonisation by appropriate wild life, such as herons, wild pigs and water buffalo. Sennacherib wished to ensure an abundant supply of water for his new palace, for which he invented a system of beams and crosspieces over wellheads with an endless bronze chain with buckets attached.

Assyriologists have debated the existence of the famous hanging gardens of Babylon, with one suggesting that they were really at Nineveh and scribal errors and tradition placed them mistakenly at Babylon.

In all probability the truth is that both Nineveh and Babylon had wonderful gardens and spectacular displays of flowers and foliage. Both Sennacherib and Nebuchadnezzar married women from distant lands who longed for the trees, hills and mountains of home.

Nebuchadnezzar was at the fall of Nineveh in 612 BC and probably saw what remained of Sennacherib's engineering feat, and eventually copied and improved on it when he became king of Babylon.

However splendid Nineveh looked when the work was completed, it would have been very strange to the modern Western eye (and nostril) for standards of hygiene were not as stringent as today.

SPECULATE TO ACCUMULATE

Sennacherib's ambitious building projects were of course made possible because he controlled vast imperial resources. He was the son and successor of Sargon and as crown prince had been entrusted by his father with positions of responsibility in different parts of the empire. He therefore came to the throne as an experienced administrator and soldier, and as legitimate successor was in a position to take firm hold of his inheritance, which extended from the Egyptian border to well inside Asia Minor and from north-west Iran to the Persian Gulf.

Wherever he went he was on the lookout for new ideas and more slaves: 'the enemy population which my hand has conquered' were forced to work on his palace.

When new palaces were completed, the gods of Assyria were invited inside (probably meaning that statues of gods were moved into various shrines). However, Sennacherib left one God out of his life and it would cost him dearly.

A COMMON MISTAKE

Across the world today there are many empire builders, both large and small. The pursuit for the accumulation of wealth, power and property goes on at an alarming rate, and the weak, infirm and underprivileged are often pushed to one side or downtrodden in the rush for gain. Jesus sent out a clear warning, 'Watch out! Be on your guard against all kinds of greed; a man's life does not consist in the abundance of his possessions' (Luke 12:15).

Jesus also warned that in the light of eternity what would it profit anyone if they gained the whole world and lost their own soul (Matthew 16:26)?

FOR FURTHER STUDY

1. In Isaiah 66, a description is given of the life to come. What other Old Testament prophets describe the future hope of the believer?
2. Jesus, in John 14:1–6, gives an outline of what he will be doing when he has ascended back to heaven. From the New Testament letters, can you find other descriptions of his present activity, and write out why they are important?

TO THINK ABOUT AND DISCUSS

1. *Sennacherib built for himself a great city and lavish premises in which to live. Is it wrong for Christians to own fine houses and live in luxury, when there is so much poverty and need in the world?*
2. *The environment is under constant threat due to the encroachment of man, so how can sensible living conditions be maintained without it being detrimental to the surrounding areas. Also, what penalties should be in place to deter the greedy speculator?*
3. *What are the full implications of the obligations God laid on mankind in Genesis 1:28–30?*

Note

1   **Arthur Ferrill,** *The Origins of War* (Thames and Hudson), p. 77.

7 King of the ends of the earth

Isaiah 52, 53

With tail between his legs, Sennacherib returned to Nineveh and became immersed in various building projects, after that he renewed his campaigning, but in a different field of operations.

HAS THE BIBLE MADE A MISTAKE?

A plain reading of the Bible would lead the unwary to think that as soon as he returned home Sennacherib died, but there is a gap of almost nineteen years between 2 Kings 36–37, 2 Chronicles 32:21a–21b, and Isaiah 37:37–38.

Although the Scriptures are silent on the years 700–681 BC, it does not mean that God lost interest in Sennacherib. A prophet of that time wrote, 'He has showed you, O man, what is good. And what does the LORD require of you? To act justly and to love mercy and to walk humbly with your God' (Micah 6:8).

A stay of execution was given to Sennacherib by God so that he could not only reflect on what had happened, but also, like *King Ashur-dan III* when Jonah came to Nineveh, repent in sackcloth and dust (Jonah 3:6).

Although the Bible is quiet regarding these intervening

years, the work of archaeologists and historians has shed light on the king's activities, and sadly they do not show a man who took Micah's words to heart.

The value of studying biblical history is that it fills in the events that the Bible leaves out. For the Bible is a specialist book; it deals with God, man, sin and salvation and how God brings sinners to repentance and then to glory. So it must, by its very nature, be selective in it what it records. Never succumb to the theory that there are mistakes in the Bible, for it is God's holy word and speaks without error concerning all that is recorded (2 Timothy 3:16).

So what was Sennacherib up to before God judged him with death?

SOMEONE WILL PAY FOR THIS

Humility was a commodity in short supply in the life of this man, for Sennacherib, like all dictators, delighted in promoting himself. Among the many inscriptions he left is the following:

'Sennacherib the glorious, terror of nations, King of the Earth's Four Corners, Lord of the Earth, King of kings.'

Throughout the reign of Sennacherib, the greatest problems were in Babylonia; the handling of that country was a perennial problem for Assyrian kings. It was so closely linked with Assyria by culture, geography and trade that the situation in one inevitably affected the other. Assyria had the military power but Babylonia was held in high esteem as the homeland of the common culture; Assyrian kings, for example, including Sennacherib, wrote their inscriptions not in their own Assyrian dialect (used for their letters) but in Babylonian.

Sargon had been very gentle with the Babylonian cities, and Sennacherib at first attempted the same policy.

Two particular factors affected good order in Babylonia— Chaldaean tribesmen, mainly in the south of the country, and the ancient kingdom of Elam to the east. As we saw in Chapter 1, in 703 BC one of the Chaldaean chiefs, Merodach-Baladan (of 2 Kings 20:12) rebelled, with support from Elam. Sennacherib acted against this with temporary success, devastating the Chaldaean areas, but the trouble recurred after his Palestinian campaign. He had formerly attempted to govern the country through a native Babylonian puppet king; now he installed his own oldest son as king of Babylon in an attempt to achieve Assyrian control with the minimum use of military force. This was frustrated by the increasing involvement of Elam.

Earlier, Elam had provided Merodach-Baladan with military assistance, and it was now giving the Chaldaean tribes a safe base east of the Persian Gulf, to which they could withdraw when pursued by Sennacherib. The security of the Babylonian cities could not be assured while Chaldaean tribes were able to raid with impunity. Sennacherib used his inventiveness to plan an elaborate amphibious operation to overcome this problem. He brought skilled shipwrights from the Mediterranean coast to build ships at Nineveh. From there they were sailed down the Tigris to near where Baghdad now stands, transported overland to a canal leading to the more easily navigable Euphrates, and then sailed down to the Persian Gulf. Sennacherib then shipped his cavalry and infantry to the other side of the Gulf, where they destroyed the Chaldaean bases and captured some Elamite cities.

This produced an escalation of hostilities, and in 694 BC Elam made a counter-attack against Assyrian interests in Babylonia, taking prisoner Sennacherib's son Ashur-nãdin-sumi, and appointing an Elamite nominee to the throne of Babylon. This brought war between pro-Elamite and pro-Assyrian elements in Babylonia, with increasing chaos, which doubtless added to the unpopularity of the Assyrians as the occupying power. Even in the cities, which were traditionally pro-Assyrian, strong pro-Elamite factions developed, and eventually Babylon itself sent its temple treasures to buy Elamite military aid against Sennacherib. Elam responded, which led to a battle in 691 BC with appalling carnage on both sides. The Elamite army was broken and unable to oppose Sennacherib for the remainder of his reign, and Sennacherib himself had to return home to regroup.

THE DILEMMA WITH BABYLON

The anti-Assyrian stance of Babylon had now convinced Sennacherib that to achieve a solution in Babylonia he had to destroy the capital. In 689 BC he moved south with this objective. His operation was thorough. Sennacherib took Babylon by siege and 'overwhelmed it like a hurricane'.

Because his son had disappeared, possibly murdered in Susa, Sennacherib focused his ultimate ferocity on the great Temple of Marduk, the chief god of Babylon. The ruthless destruction and desecration of this temple made him infamous, as he carried off the god's statue to Nineveh. Also he filled the open spaces with corpses, shared out all valuables as booty for his troops, smashed statues of the gods and confiscated temple property, demolished houses, temples and city walls, and dug canals across the whole city to flood it. He even had the soil of the city thrown into the Euphrates to be carried down to the sea. Finally he set up memorial stelas to record what he had done. All this made such a wide impression that the people of Dilmun (Bahrain) in the Persian Gulf, six hundred miles from Babylon, sent tribute as a token of submission.

REVERTING TO TYPE

The experiences in Judah had not changed this man; he was still a formidable warrior, and had proved to his people that he could strike decisively against a capital city. His inscriptions show a growing confidence in his ability to remain unchallenged. In earlier texts he was known as 'The pious shepherd, fearful of the great gods'. After 697 BC he became 'expert shepherd, favourite of the great gods'.

WHAT OF HEZEKIAH AND JUDAH?

Although Sennacherib was gone he was not forgotten. Many reports would have come with the merchants travelling to and from Jerusalem, and the diplomatic corps would have been up to speed with his exploits.

Although it is not possible to give a precise date to the writing of Isaiah 40 and 41, it may have been from this time. For undoubtedly the Hebrews had under God won a great victory over the Assyrian menace. But that wounded lion would now be even more dangerous, and who could say whether or not he would return to vent his fury against them? King Hezekiah died in 687 BC, six years before Sennacherib, and that may have destabilised Judah, for although his son

Manasseh ruled, he was very different to his father. Sennacherib may have been tempted to look west again in the hope that he could be successful now that a new king was on the throne.

Isaiah, in chapters 40 and 41, speaks words of comfort to those who are not feeling comfortable. If these words had been composed before this time, it is of no consequence for the word of God is timeless and those who were fearful should have gained great comfort from the fact that God 'gives strength to the weary' (Isaiah 40:29), and he is 'the LORD, your God, who takes hold of your right hand and says to you, Do not fear; I will help you' (Isaiah 41:13).

John Calvin helpfully said, 'whenever we are attacked by any severe contest, let us learn to look to him; for if we hesitate and look hither and thither, we shall never enjoy peace of mind.'[1]

I AM WITH YOU

Isaiah reminded the people that God knew all about Sennacherib's activities:

For this is what the Sovereign LORD says, 'At first my people went down to Egypt to live; lately, Assyria has oppressed them. And now what do I have here?' declares the LORD. 'For my people have been taken away for nothing, and those who rule them mock,' declares the LORD.

'And all day long my name is constantly blasphemed. Therefore my people will know my name; therefore in that day they will know that it is I who foretold it. Yes, it is I.'

Isaiah 52:4–6

According to the writings and carvings that have been discovered, it seems that seasoned Assyrian soldiers loved to torture and maim. It may be an unfair assessment to consider them the most bloodthirsty nation of the ancient world as so little is known about the practices of surrounding peoples. But in all probability, if they worked to type, outside the walls of Jerusalem as at the siege of Lachish, prisoners would have been brought forward and impaled on stakes before the horrified gaze of the inhabitants of Jerusalem, as a stark visual aid of what awaited those who resisted the demands of Sennacherib.

THE SUFFERING SERVANT

These events form the background to Isaiah's wonderful prophecy regarding the deliverer who would come. Not another Hezekiah to save the people from a Sennacherib, but one greater then Hezekiah: the suffering servant who would save all of God's people from sin and Satan.

Isaiah was to foretell that this saviour (Jesus means saviour) would seven hundred years later be lifted up outside the walls of Jerusalem. But to many it seemed incredible that the coming Messiah was to suffer in such an awful way for the sins of the world (Isaiah 52:13–53:12).

FOR FURTHER STUDY

1. While it is not imperative to understand every historical character, some background knowledge of their life can enhance the Bible study. For example, in Luke 2 we read about Caesar Augustus, who issued a decree that a census be taken of the entire Roman world. Using books, the Internet, or both, what can you learn about that

man, and how does it enhance your knowledge of the world that
Jesus entered?

2. Paul also used to refer to current situations to enhance his
preaching. For one example read Acts 17:28. Can you find others in
the New Testament?

TO THINK ABOUT AND DISCUSS

1. If the statement was made, 'the Bible is full of errors', how could
you show it to be false?

2. The early chapters of 1 Chronicles in the Old Testament are taken
up with listing name after name. Why has God permitted all the
names to be recorded, and what benefit can they be to a twenty-first
century reader?

3. Does having a grasp of history and current events help in
encouraging Christians who are persecuted or struggling with life?

4. What other verses from Isaiah 40 and 41 can be used to bring
comfort to the weary or persecuted?

5. What amazing statements are made about the Messiah in Isaiah
53, and how did Jesus fulfil each one of them?

Note

1   **John Calvin,** *Commentary on the Prophet Isaiah,* volume III (Grand Rapids:
    Baker Book House), p. 260.

8 A stab in the dark

2 Kings 19:35–37; 2 Chronicles 32:21; Isaiah 37:37

Death waited in the dark as the great king stood in the temple of his god. He had come to offer appropriate sacrifices and to receive the god's blessings on his future plans. Then a sudden noise behind him, followed by a blow from a sword, ended not only his hopes but also his life.

ACTION AND REACTION

What led to this dramatic line of action being taken?

In 694 BC, Sennacherib's eldest son and heir-designate, Ashur-nãdin-sumi (possibly the one standing in front of the enthroned Sennacherib on the Lachish reliefs), was captured by Babylonians and carried off to Elam; he is not heard of again. Some think that he was strangled with a bowstring in the dungeons at Susa, a despicable end for the son of a king.

The second-eldest son, Adrammelech (*Arda-Mulissi*), now has every reason to expect to be the next crown prince; however, he is out-manoeuvred from this position in favour of Esarhaddon. The younger brother of Adrammelech becomes the favourite son of Sennacherib thanks to his powerful mother, Naqi'a-Zakutu, who crucially is not the mother of Adrammelech. Eventually, Esarhaddon is officially proclaimed crown prince, and all Assyria is made to swear allegiance to him. However, Adrammelech enjoys considerable popularity among certain circles who would like to see him as their future king rather than sickly, superstitious Esarhaddon. As the years pass, the opposition to Esarhaddon grows, while at the same time Adrammelech and his brother(s) gain in popularity. This political development leads to a turn of events, but not to the one hoped for by Adrammelech and his supporters. Foreseeing trouble, Sennacherib sends Esarhaddon away from the capital to the western provinces; yet he does not revise the order of succession.

In this situation, Adrammelech and his brother(s) soon find themselves in a stalemate. On the one hand, they are at their political zenith while their rival brother has to languish in exile; on the other hand, the latter remains the crown prince, and there is nothing his brothers can do about it since Esarhaddon has been moved beyond their grasp and is out of reach in the provinces.

I WILL NOT CHANGE MY MIND!

Sennacherib's mind remains unchanged, but if Esarhaddon was able to score military victories, his popularity would undoubtedly rise while that of his brothers might easily start to sink. The only way for them to make good the situation, is to act swiftly and take over the kingship by force.

Babylonian influence was so strong in Assyria that for centuries there had been pro-Babylonian elements in high places. Sennacherib's sacrilegious sack of Babylon must have aroused opposition in Assyria as well as in Babylonia.

So it was that Sennacherib is stabbed to death in the temple of his god Nisroch by Adrammelech and Sharezer (only named in the Bible, he may have been *Sar-etir-Assur*, a known son of Sennacherib), near a winged bull colossus guarding the temple where he had been praying.

Sennacherib's son Esarhaddon wrote of this outrage to Assyrian ideals:

They plotted evil, they rejected the gods above. They revolted, to gain the kingship they slew Sennacherib, their father.

Many years later, when subduing a rebellion in Babylon, Sennacherib's grandson, King Ashurbanipal, makes reference to this event:

As for those men and their vulgar mouths, who uttered vulgarity against Ashur, my god, and plotted evil against me, the prince who fears him, I slit their mouths and brought them low. The rest of the people, by the colossi, between which they had cut down, Sennacherib, the father of the father who begot me, I cut down those people there, as an offering to his shade.

Concerning the place where Sennacherib was slain, 'the temple of his god Nisroch' (2 Kings 19:37), Jeremy Black and Anthony Green write: 'It is not clear to which Assyrian god this refers; it has been suggested that it is a corruption of Ninurta, but this is unsubstantiated.'[1]

AN INTERESTING TRADITION?

A fascinating account of Sennacherib's last day is given in the extra-biblical writings of ancient Jewish rabbis and recorded in Louis Ginzberg's, *Legends of the Jews*. It says that, on his return to Assyria, Sennacherib found a plank, which he had worshipped as an idol, because it was part of the ark that had saved Noah from the deluge. He vowed that he would sacrifice to this idol if he prospered in his next ventures. But his sons heard his vows and they killed their father and fled to Kardu where they released Jewish captives confined there in great numbers.

If this tradition is true then it is rather ironic that his murderers escaped to the land of Ararat, the very place where the ark alighted after the great worldwide flood had abated. But if that is so then it is a sad reflection on Sennacherib that, like many others throughout history, he worshipped created things rather then the creator (Revelation 19:10).

The date of Sennacherib's death was 20 of the month Tebet (December/January) 681 BC; an inscription marking Sennacherib's tomb was found at the city of Ashur.

KING AND COMMONER ALL THE SAME AT LAST

For all his pomp and circumstance, Sennacherib had to taste the bitterness of mortality and the sting of death. He had no comfort in death; did he look into the eyes of his son as his life ebbed away? The news of the murder of Sennacherib was received with mixed feelings but certainly with strong emotion all over the ancient Near East. In Judah and Babylonia it was hailed as godsent punishment for the 'godless' deeds of a hated despot; in Assyria, the reaction must have been one of overwhelming horror and resentment. Not surprisingly, then, the event is relatively well reported or referred to in contemporary and later sources, both cuneiform and non-cuneiform.

For all his pompous boasting, Sennacherib could do nothing

to stop his body returning to the dust, being buried in the royal mausoleum at the holy city of Ashur.

FOR FURTHER STUDY

1. History is full of examples of the good and the great who thought they would live for ever. How many examples in the Bible can you find of people who thought that death would not catch up with them?
2. Surrounded by many who are sceptical towards Christianity, what verses in the Bible would you use to challenge their stance?

TO THINK ABOUT AND DISCUSS

1. Jesus said that even though you owned the whole world, its value is less then a human soul. Do you think he was just using exaggerated language to make a point? If not, how should we understand his words in Matthew 16:26?
2. Many people spend a great deal of money on funerals and a wake. Is that a wise use of funds, or is there a better way to remember the dead?
3. Many ancient graves are visited and sometimes the bones or bodies are put on view. Is there any justification for such actions or should a greater respect be shown to the dead?
4. Some Christians think that it is wrong to cremate the body and where possible all should be buried. Why do you think some hold to this view and can one mode be shown to be superior to another?

Note

1   **Jeremy Black** and **Anthony Green,** *Gods, Demons and Symbols of Ancient Mesopotamia*, (London: British Museum Press), p. 143.

9 Loss of face

2 Chronicles 32:21

Recording events, the historian wrote in 2 Chronicles 32:21b that Sennacherib withdrew to his own land in disgrace, literally 'in shame of face'.[1] He had failed in his objective and it made him a figure of scorn among the nations.

THE GREAT KING LOSES FACE, AGAIN!

As we have already seen, Sennacherib himself took part in the siege at Lachish and is depicted receiving the defeated prisoners as he sits upon his high throne. The inscription above and to the left of him reads, 'Sennacherib King of the world, King of Assyria, on a seat he sat and the booty of Lachish before him it passed.' No one could ever accuse him of false humility!

The king's chariot and bodyguard are below and behind him; however, the king's face has been hacked out—perhaps the vengeful work of a Babylonian soldier when Nineveh itself was destroyed in 612 BC.

To lose face in the ancient world meant that not only was the king disfigured and defaced, but that his memory was being expunged; it would be as though he never existed.

SENNACHERIB LOST FACE AS A COMMANDER

Unlike the British monarch today, the Assyrian king held

absolute sway over targets, deployment and tactics when his army went to war. He would take advice but the final decision was always his. It seems today that many still follow him in thinking that they run their own little empires either at home, work, in church or the world at large. As with Sennacherib, the reality is so different, for none is master of his own destiny. He lost face in the campaign that was meant to enhance his reputation but left him diminished, for he had to withdraw from Judah without securing the total dominance over the land that he desired. This must have rankled, for previous Assyrian kings, Tiglath-Pileser III, Shalmaneser V, and his father Sargon II, had come against the Northern Kingdom of Israel and not only defeated it but also deported the population who never returned to their homeland.

These historical events are seen in the contrasts that have come down to us today. In the Bible there is a brief mention about Lachish, whereas Sennacherib devotes a whole room to it, and in the Bible there is a large amount about Jerusalem, whereas Sennacherib gives it little space by comparison. Sin always magnifies the wrong thing and tries to exalt what is insignificant. How great a distance there is between Sennacherib and the Lord Jesus Christ, who is called in Joshua 5:15, 'The commander of the Lord's army'! For the Lord always leads his people as the one who alone brings stability and everlasting peace: 'But thanks be to God, who always leads us in triumphal procession in Christ' (2 Corinthians 2:14a).

SENNACHERIB LOST FACE AS A FATHER

It is a terrible thing when children have little or no respect for their father. Sennacherib's sons turned on him. He did not realise the danger that lay within his own household: he would have been wise to have kept his sons close to him. As princes of the royal household they would probably have been trained in the art of war, and part of their training meant learning not to fear the enemy or any foreign god. Thus two of his sons, Adrammelech and Sharezer, learnt the art of dispassionate warfare. It emboldened them and they cut him down with the sword in the temple of his god Nisroch.

Whatever his sons' grievance, the fact is that Sennacherib had lost face with them. The bigger picture is shown in the Bible as it clearly links his death to the events at Jerusalem in 701 BC, almost twenty years before. God had given Sennacherib ample time to repent and turn from his ways, but when he did not, judgement fell on him and it was those who should have been closest to him who dealt the final blows. God is often patient towards sinners, but just because judgement is not always immediate does not mean that people have escaped, for God graciously waits for repentance. But as with Sennacherib, time eventually runs out. That is why the Bible urges action and all need to repent and believe while there is still time.

A MODERN EXAMPLE

Those who set themselves up in opposition to the only true and living God will always come unstuck and, like Sennacherib, lose face.

In recent times we have seen and heard a great deal about the dictator Saddam Hussein, former President of Iraq, who ruled in the land familiar to Sennacherib. Yet as the days go by our news bulletins are no longer so concerned with him, and although his trial and execution thrust him into the public eye, all it did was show that his empire was just a transitory thing. Many in the Arab world were shocked to see him undergoing a medical check-up after his capture, and one report said, 'It shows he has lost face.'

A RUDE AWAKENING

Sennacherib thought of himself as being invincible and one inscription calls him, *'Great King, mighty King, King of the universe, King of the country of Ashur.'* But how must he have felt at the moment his spirit left his body?

What terror seized Sennacherib as he realised that the gods of Assyria were figments of the imagination and the one true God was the one he had challenged and now had to face (Hebrews 9:27)?

Was he permitted to see just how small his empire truly was, as his spirit returned to God (Ecclesiastes 12:7)? Did God allow him a view of the full extent of Asia, Africa and then across the oceans to the Americas, Australasia and to Antarctica, lands he knew nothing about? By contrast, how feeble his empire was shown to have been. What thoughts filled his mind as he was ushered out into the echoing vaults of eternity and to the waiting place for unbelieving departed spirits, Hades (Luke 16:23), until the dawn of the day of judgement?

THE IMPERATIVE ISSUE

Without doubt, the most important question anyone can ask is this: 'Who is God and how can I know him?' The Bible says that only Jesus has the answer to that question and if we do not listen to him, then our path leads to destruction (Matthew 7:13). He alone can be trusted and he is the only one who has never lost face. As the apostle Paul wrote in 2 Corinthians 4:6, 'For God, who said, "Let light shine out of darkness," made his light shine in our hearts to give us the light of the knowledge of the glory of God in the face of Christ.'

FOR FURTHER STUDY

1. Read about the humiliation of Miriam, Moses' sister, in Numbers 12.
2. Look at Psalm 14 to see God's estimation of the foolish.

TO THINK ABOUT AND DISCUSS

1. Most people like to be well thought of and hate to be embarrassed. Should Christians ever deliberately humiliate anyone?
2. Many crimes remain unsolved. Thinking about the delay in Sennacherib's judgement, should the church be more active in preaching repentance before it is too late for the sinner to turn to God for forgiveness?
3. At the Last Supper, Jesus said that it would have been better if Judas had never been born (Matthew 26:24). What emotions do you think Judas experienced before he committed suicide? (See Matthew 27:1–5; Acts 1:18,19.)
4. How do you think those who Jesus describes as goats (Matthew 25:31–46) will feel when they are assigned to their eternal position?

Note

1 **Allan Harman,** *Isaiah a covenant to be kept for the sake of the church* (Fearn, Tain: Christian Focus), p. 253.

10 History's verdict

2 Chronicles 32:22–23

'Historians like a quiet life, and usually they get it. For the most part, history moves at a deliberate pace, working its changes subtly and incrementally. Nations and their institutions harden into shape or crumble away like sediment carried by the flow of a sluggish river.'[1]

ASHES TO ASHES, DUST TO DUST

Sennacherib's life must have seemed like a whirlwind to those who were caught up in his maelstrom, but his reign laid the foundations for the collapse and disappearance of the Assyrians from the face of the earth. One Assyriologist has written, 'Sennacherib stands out, among Assyrian kings, as a man of exceptional enterprise and open-mindedness.' Yet for all his achievements he is largely forgotten or unknown today, and pales into insignificance next to Nebuchadnezzar, even though his achievements were from a human standpoint as striking as that great king of Babylon. The reason for this is not hard to understand, for the total devastation of the Assyrian empire is one of the best lessons in modesty that the ancient world can provide.

Dante, in the second part of his *Divine Comedy* which he based on the fictitious place of Purgatory, places Sennacherib at the level of pride.[2] This is a good assessment, for the king was a proud man.

Sennacherib was a mighty man, feared, revered and

honoured in his lifetime, but still he ended up in the grave, buried in the city of Ashur, which now lies—like him—forgotten by many, ruined and ravaged by time.

GOD'S MAN

A very deliberate distinction between Sennacherib and Hezekiah is made in the Bible as Hezekiah's subsequent standing in the world due to God's hand being upon him is clearly shown (2 Chronicles 32:22–23).

In the New Testament, the greatest of conquerors was laid to rest in a tomb by one of his followers but he did not remain in it. The bones of the Lord Jesus Christ have not turned to dust, for he did not remain in the tomb but rose again on the third day and lives for ever. In speaking of his triumph, Jesus says: 'Do not be afraid … I am the Living One; I was dead, and behold I am alive for ever and ever! And I hold the keys of death and Hades' (Revelation 1:17).

LESSONS TO LEARN

What are the eternal lessons that arise from a study of Sennacherib's opposition to the almighty God?

• GOD PROTECTS THOSE WHO TRUST IN HIM

He is a shield to his people when they call to him for help. At the close of the Assyrian empire, Nahum gave reassurance that the Lord is someone who not only knows his people but takes care of them (Nahum 1:7).

• GOD HONOURS THOSE WHO WORSHIP HIM IN TRUTH

Many false religions abound, but all of them have this one

thing in common: they are reflections or make-overs of the serpent's words, 'Did God really say?' (Genesis 3:1). A questioning of God and his word and the subsequent unbelief lead many down the broad road to destruction that Jesus warned against (Matthew 7:13).

• GOD HUMBLES THE SINNER

The Rabshakeh thought he held all the trump cards and that Hezekiah and Jerusalem were just like fruit on a tree ripe for devouring. Yet he foolishly left one important factor out of his calculations: that the God of the Hebrews is the one and only true and living God. It was he who had permitted Assyria to rise, expand and become the rod of his chastening (Isaiah 7:17–20).

• GOD JUDGES FOOLISH WORDS

Of the many recorded sayings of Jesus one of the most frightening is, 'I tell you that men will have to give account on the day of judgment for every careless word they have spoken' (Matthew 12:36). The Rabshakeh, on behalf of Sennacherib, had spoken careless words thinking that diplomatic speech was beyond criticism, but he was sadly mistaken. Everybody needs to remember this that is why the following prayer was made: 'Set a guard over my mouth, O LORD; keep watch over the door of my lips' (Psalm 141:3).

• GOD OVERTHROWS THOSE WHO RESIST HIM

Anyone who takes on God is in an unfair contest, for if God chooses to he will simply outlive his enemy and then where will they be? In eternity with no one to help them. How rightly the

Scripture says, 'It is a dreadful thing to fall into the hands of the living God' (Hebrews 10:31).

ALMIGHTY POWER!

Sennacherib offered Judah protection and peace, but it was a lie. He tried to bring increasing troubles on a troubled mind, but Hezekiah, with Isaiah's help, stood firm. The Assyrians would never be happy until their rule dominated, and when they did not get their way, they waged war and destroyed all opponents. Ultimately this mighty nation tried to destroy God's chosen people but was itself destroyed. Those who remained in Jerusalem, who refused the invitations to bargain away their steadfast convictions, found absolute protection under almighty God.[3]

Confronted by the might of the Assyrian empire, its military prowess, and the Assyrian reputation for brutality, some would undoubtedly have considered surrender. They would see the Assyrian power as invincible. In such times strong godly leadership is required and that is what King Hezekiah and Isaiah the prophet provided in answer to the prayers that were offered up to heaven. Today, when confronted by those opposed to God's laws, to the Lord Jesus and his people, criticising them and seeking to undermine their every effort, what should be done? When this question is asked, listen to Hezekiah's exhortation and learn from it:

'Be strong and courageous. Do not be afraid or discouraged because of the king of Assyria and the vast army with him, for there is a greater power with us than with him. With him is only the arm of flesh, but with us is the LORD our God to help us and to fight our battles' (2 Chronicles 32:7–8).

FOR FURTHER STUDY

1. *'Be strong and courageous' is a phrase that is used at key times throughout the Bible. Locate each usage and, considering the context, write out why these words were spoken at a given time.*
2. *Jesus often called people to live courageously for him. What passages in the Gospels speak of his call to faithful discipleship?*

TO THINK ABOUT AND DISCUSS

1. *How should Christians respond today to the many challenges to their faith?*
2. *If an unbelieving friend were in trouble, what scriptures would you share with them and why?*
3. *Sennacherib's invasion of Judah has been documented three times, in 2 Kings, 2 Chronicles and Isaiah. Now that you have considered these passages, why do you think God has seen fit to record them so often?*
4. *What do you think is the overall message of these passages, and what lessons would you draw from them to help Christians to live God-honouring lives?*

Notes

1 **Simon Schama,** *A History of Britain 1, 3000 BC–AD 1603, At the Edge of the World* (London: BBC Worldwide Limited), p. 63.

2 **Dante Alighieri,** *The Divine Comedy 2, Purgatory* (Harmondsworth: Penguin Classics), p. 159.

3 **Dale Ralph Davis,** *2 Kings, The power and the fury* (Fearn, Tain: Christian Focus Publications), pp. 289–290.

11 Assyrian king list

The list below puts Sennacherib in an historical framework to enable the student to see where he came in history's great procession.

Assyrian kings began to extend their territory during the eighteenth century BC under Samsi-Adad, but we will begin at the time when Assyria asserted itself as a major power during the reigns of Asa in Judah and Baasha in Israel.

King	BC	Significant events
Tukulti-Ninurta II	890–884	The reigns of Asa and Baasha, kings of Judah and Israel.
Ashurnasirpal II	883–859	The time of Ahab, king of Israel and the prophets Elijah and Elisha
Shalmaneser III	859–824	His records mention subduing Ahab.
Shamsi-Adad V	823–811	The reigns of Joash and Jehu, kings of Judah and Israel.
Adad-nirari III	810–782	Probably the deliverer in 2 Kings 13:5.
Shalmaneser IV	782–773	During the reigns of Amaziah and Jeroboam II.
Ashur-dan III	772–754	Probably king when Jonah went to Nineveh.
Ashur-nirari V	754–744	During the reigns of Azariah and Menahem.
Tiglath-pileser III	744–727	2 Kings 15:29 (also the Pul of v.19)

Shalmaneser V	727–722	2 Kings 17:3–6
Sargon II	722–705	Isaiah 20:1
Sennacherib	704–681	2 Kings 18:13
Esarhaddon	680–669	2 Kings 19:37
Ashurbanipal	669–627	Ezra 4:10

End of Assyria with the fall of Nineveh to Babylonians and Medes in 612 BC.[14]

Note

1 **Brian Edwards** and **Clive Anderson,** *Through the British Museum with the Bible* (Leominster: Day One, 2004), p. 84.